The Inspiration Code

Secrets of unlocking your people's potential

TERRY HILL

The Inspiration Code

First published in 2016 by

Panoma Press Ltd
48 St Vincent Drive, St Albans, Herts, AL1 5SJ, UK
info@panomapress.com
www.panomapress.com

Book design and layout by Neil Coe.

Printed on acid-free paper from managed forests.

ISBN 978-1-784520-82-3

"Morale is low... as usual."

"My people want more money and promotions but
I can't give either."

"I pay my staff well but most leave within two
years."

"I gave my star performer everything, she still left...
and for a lesser job!"

"I cannot inspire my team to step up in the face of
tough competition."

"We need to transform our game but the guys just
don't get it."

"I'd love to be a transformational leader but I'm not
really that charismatic."

"One negative member of my team is dragging
everyone down."

"I'm confused by all the motivation theories out
there. Just give me something that works."

Testimonials

"Every so often a book comes along that you just can't put down, a book that changes the way you see the world. Terry Hill has crafted such a book with this challenging, informative and above all practical roadmap to help you navigate through the tricky field of leading both yourself and others."

Steve Clarke,
Commercial Director, Pharmaceutical Industry

"The Inspiration Code is a valuable guide for leaders of teams who are looking for ways to build consistent high performance. Terry draws on his experience and expertise in this area to skilfully cover many insightful aspects of motivation in a way that is readily accessible and encourages practical application by the reader."

Graham Franklin,
former Director of Sales

"This easy-to-read-in-one-sitting book will take you on a practical, thought challenging yet reassuring trek through the minefield of motivational theories to lead you to the holy grail of 'thank heavens for the choice of pragmatic solutions I can really get my head around and use' moment!"

**Sandra Whitehead,
Director of Training**

"An accessible and informative read, with a set of easy-to-apply tools for today's busy leaders. I would recommend this to anyone who wants to understand what drives people to achieve higher performance, and how they can accomplish this."

**David Bobs,
National Training Manager**

Acknowledgments

A few thanks are in order for this book. I begin with my tutor Matthew Jellis at University of Worcester who supported me with the original research project that ultimately led here.

For the production I was fortunate to have not one but two amazing book coaches in Mindy Gibbins-Klein and Kate Keenan. Through their fantastic know-how and regular prodding, I actually got things done to plan, to a higher standard and on time.

I mustn't forget Barbara my dear wife for all her valued support and patience during this time.

Some of my corporate colleagues deserve a special mention, particularly Steve Clarke, Graham Franklin, J C Barland, Sandra Whitehead, David Bobs, Sandra Du Cros, Brian Green and Fiona Mack.

These guys had all the experience and expertise to help me ensure it was all readable, practical and actually helpful for all you leaders out there finding your way through the minefield that is motivation.

Thanks everyone!

Terry

Foreword by Steve Clarke, Commercial Director
Pharmaceutical Industry

For the past 30 years in progressively more senior commercial roles I have had the pleasure of working alongside many great people as both a leader and a follower... and both can be equally difficult! The one thing both activities have in common, however, is the unleashing of *potential* when both leadership and 'followership' combine. To my mind, leaders must obsess about one thing: the realisation of what can be and how to turn an individual's and a team's potential into reality!

There's nothing wrong with being a manager, indeed managers are required more than ever in dealing with today's challenges. However, they deal with today whereas leaders focus on tomorrow and search for ways to unlock the potential that exists in themselves, their teams and ultimately the environment they are working in. Failure to focus on what could be means people stand still and if people stand still businesses don't progress.

Terry has managed to create that rare thing – a book that will challenge the way you look at yourself and those that you work alongside. If on your leadership travels you are used to looking out of the window at the way others are behaving, this book will challenge you to look in the mirror first and take stock of your own actions to understand how best to unleash the potential in others.

Enjoy the Journey!

Steve

Preface

How this book came about

Thank you for choosing this book. Its roots go back to the late 1970s. As a new psychology graduate wanting to inspire others, I spent two agonising years in teaching. Motivating reluctant teenagers is still the hardest job I know. I moved quickly into retail management and even more quickly into pharmaceuticals where I held a number of sales, management, training and coaching roles in some market-leading organisations.

The pharma industry was a truly inspirational place to be. We were well paid, well treated and we could really make a difference. I worked with some great people managers but alas some that just didn't get it. The bad guys were much fewer and usually weeded out, but their impact was profound and lasting. They taught me what not to do with my people.

Motivation is one of those elusive things that even the most enlightened companies get wrong. Great leaders know it's the soft stuff that really counts. But hard data pushes out soft data and the job of getting the troops onside gets shelved. More urgent but less important business takes priority. Meanwhile the cost of workplace disengagement is huge and the most effective remedies cost little.

I saw the human cost of getting it wrong when it was easier to get it right.

I've seen the cost of employees who were passively or even actively disengaged – effectively saboteurs in their own organisations. I've seen the trails of destruction they leave and those of the managers that created them. I witnessed incentive schemes that only sowed discord, goal-setting exercises that crushed the will to work, formal appraisal systems that set colleagues against each other, employee engagement surveys that failed to capture what was really important. We now know much better.

Having made my mark in sales and uncomfortable with formal authority, I sought leadership positions that depended on persuasion rather than position. My most enjoyable and successful role was in performance coaching. There I learned that the motivation behind peak performance is never something we do unto others. The most powerful motivation comes from the inside, waiting to be unlocked by the leader that holds the right mindset and asks the right questions.

Eventually the job I loved changed. I burned out as my role became less aligned to my abilities, more procedural, and more meaningless. Having always told others to follow their hearts and play to their strengths, I now needed to walk the talk. So I left to start an MSc in Work Psychology and to set up my own company. Passionate about those things that drive our behaviour, my aim was to make a difference to people like me and help change workplaces for the better. Unimpressed by the practicality of motivation theories, I forged some well-tried and tested techniques from Performance Coaching, Neuro Linguistic Programming (NLP) and Positive Psychology into the Motive Mapping method that I describe and advocate. I researched the methods' effectiveness for uncovering powerful internal motivators that lead to greater work engagement and health.

Why read this book?

Here is an inside-out programme for uncovering, igniting and harnessing the inner passions of each and every member of your team. Follow it and you can make your workplace a more inspirational, productive and healthier place to be. Both you and your team will win. You'll get the complete toolkit for success.

I won't be giving a detailed account of classic and modern motivation models and theories. I review their place in the current scheme of things, but we really have more than enough of these. We just need to get cleverer with what we have. We need to turn what science knows into something useful and practical, into techniques that can be applied to any situation, group or individual to get a result.

With the right mindset and tools, inspiration becomes the norm. This book is short. It gets quickly to what's really important. I will draw on important research but prefer to engage you the reader with self-evident principles and real world examples: what goes wrong, why it goes wrong and how to get it right. So enjoy the stories and the insights, relate them to your own experience, do the exercises and test the toolkit. Each chapter takes your impact to new levels, going beyond the limitations for what came before.

We begin with those popular pieces of corporate wisdom and practices that only weigh your people down. You will find ways to lighten or even remove the burden, ways to free up your people. Next you'll find powerful principles to transform a workplace. The real power of this book lies in the sharper instruments that follow. Motive Mapping takes a truly personal approach, identifying and unlocking every individual's existing passions. You will get results with even your most difficult people. Motivating from the outside is hard work. It can be and usually is resisted. In contrast, the motivation that comes from within is almost impossible to resist because we own it.

Now you can quickly and easily capture anyone's most powerful inner motives, those that could drive peak performance. You can turn mere jobs into 'causes', causes that will create the team of outperformers you've always wanted.

Contents

Chapter 1

Your motive mindset: How well does it serve you?

The importance of maps

Imagine you are trying to find your way in a large and unfamiliar city. Your map is outdated and inaccurate. What do you do? You can work on your behaviour. By putting some real effort in, you can get lost twice as fast. You can adopt a more positive attitude. Now you don't care you are lost.

Only a new and more accurate map will get you where you want to go. Yet so many of us lead using the wrong maps. These are our personal theories of human nature, our blueprints for inspiring others. On the journey we can double our efforts and halve our results because in reality we are lost. We just don't know it.

Stephen Covey in *Principle Centred Leadership*[1] uses this example to highlight the importance of 'Paradigms' or 'Mental Maps'. He puts it this way:

"If you want to make minor improvements in your behaviour, in your relationships, then work on behaviour, work on attitude. If you want to make major improvements, quantum leaps, then work on Paradigms. Behaviour and attitudes will inevitably follow."

Our internal 'maps' of the world are a way of thinking, a mindset, how we believe the world works. Our understanding of what really drives us has changed radically over the last century. Yet organisations still cling to dated ways of thinking and never get the results they seek. Their people remain uninspired. The workers don't 'get it' because the leaders don't.

What you are aware of you can control. What you are unaware of controls you. A more inspirational leadership style begins with awareness of how you currently go about things, what you currently believe. Awareness of your current maps and their limitations is a great starting point, followed by awareness of why your people leave their jobs, through to awareness of those things that could really get them excited and make them want to outperform in their roles. That is our journey.

If you have an ineffective map for motivating others, this book will highlight that. You can choose a better one. If you already have an effective map, congratulations! This book will give you the tools to make it really work, to get results from others you never believed possible.

Generation Y are now with us in the workforce. Currently in their 20s and 30s, they are ambitious, socially confident and expect their voices to be heard. They want fulfilment, they want to make a difference and they want it now. If we fail to engage with them we become obsolete in a fast-changing workplace. But with the right mindset the outlook is promising. You might no longer know best but employees with a strong 'why' will work out the 'how' for themselves. Great leaders give their followers a strong sense of 'why'.

Can you replicate and even surpass what great leaders do? With the right maps and techniques it becomes possible… even probable.

Why motivation rules

Think of someone you know who is truly motivated at work. Far from being drained by punishing schedules, these people actually seem to draw energy and purpose from their greatest challenges, inspiring them to ever greater highs in performance and even health.

Poor motivation equals poor performance regardless of talent. In contrast, new employees lacking in knowledge and skills but with high motivation will quickly overcome their deficiencies. Hard work, self-belief and persistence almost always trump talent when results are the judge.

So the well-worn cliché that motivated employees are every organisation's greatest asset is still true and any manager's number one priority is the motivation and morale of the individuals they lead. 'How to motivate the workers' is still the perennial question for organisations. Finding the key promises to make everyone healthier, happier and more productive. Motivated employees have fewer accidents and ethical problems, plus lower absenteeism and turnover. They feel less stress, enjoy their work more and have better physical and mental health.

So can most of your people find meaning in a job so it becomes a source of enjoyment and purpose, leaving them with enough energy to enjoy their non-work lives? For most professionals it's a definite yes.

But if the workers are to get it, the leader must truly 'get it'. So do try the exercises that follow on yourself first. After all, it's hard to get someone else excited without being motivated yourself. If your current role doesn't excite, then use this book to know yourself better and find one that does. Then you'll be in a better place to attract followers. That is your purpose.

The biggest shift you can make

Incorrect and partial maps or mindsets have always hampered scientific progress[1]. Disease was once blamed on 'bad stuff' in the blood. Bloodletting was the logical treatment. It was ineffective of course because the map was wrong. This didn't stop efforts to perfect the art. If only it could be done more efficiently then better results would surely follow. Today we might hold teambuilding exercises for the bloodletting department.

Few suspected the map itself was wrong. Surgeons operated with filthy hands and with tragic results. Eventually the 'germ theory' of disease took hold and replaced the outdated thinking, opening up a whole new world of possibilities. A breakthrough typically involves a 'break with'.

Imagine trying to solve the woes of the old communist system by efficiency drives and positive attitude training. It was the system, the way of thinking that needed to change. Sometimes maps are not false but incomplete. Einstein rewrote the rules of Newtonian Physics giving us a more complete understanding of the universe. But Newtonian Physics was still good enough to land men on the moon. Likewise, older maps for motivation still work in some situations. So we still cling to them when science knows better.

Einstein said, "Our current problems cannot be solved by the same level of thinking that created them." Problems inherent in motivation with carrots and sticks will not be resolved by making the carrots crunchier and the sticks sharper. We need a new mindset, a new map.

Ask any manager what makes an outstanding employee and you'll get descriptions of mindset or attitude. Productive employees are seen as positive, open, determined and focused. So what about your own mindset for inspiring others? What do you believe makes others tick? How well does your current mindset serve you?

Four different leadership or motive mindsets have been described[1] and which have dominated the last century, starting with the earliest:

Scientific Management: (Level 1)

Assumptions: Workers make rational economic choices. Left to their own devices they will typically do as little as possible to retain their jobs and benefits.

Description: Authoritarian and controlling. You know best. You tell people where to go and what to do. You persuade them with carrots and sticks. You administer these fairly.

Human Relations: (Level 2)

Assumptions: People have not just economic but social needs: to be treated well, to be liked and respected, and to belong.

Description: Paternalistic, authoritarian but benevolent. If people do as they are told, you'll look after them. People have feelings so you treat them not just fairly but with kindness and courtesy.

Human Resource: (Level 3)

Assumptions: People have latent talent that needs nurturing.

Description: You tap into your people's talent and creativity. You value their skills, ask for opinions and delegate where appropriate. You create an environment that nurtures talent and where people can bring their full range of talents to bear on organisational goals.

Principle Centred Leadership: (Level 4)

Assumptions: People are not just resources and psychological beings but spiritual beings that require a purpose and meaningful goals.

Description: You aim to ensure that work is meaningful for employees and create synergy between the workers' goals and those of the organisation.

You ask people what's really important to them and then do your best to ensure their fulfilment through work. You ask what you can give your people so they can be happy, healthy and productive.

Which mindset is yours?

Take a look at the four descriptions. Your leadership style will derive most from the assumptions you make about what drives your people.

Which mindset or map describes you best, most of the time?

Think about your team. See the current problems and frustrations, yours and theirs. How might they have come about? What role could your current map have played?

So how well does your current mindset serve you? If your map is failing, you will experience lots of dilemmas; you want two things but can only achieve one at the expense of the other.

Do you find yourself having to choose between:

- Satisfying your boss and satisfying your subordinates?

- Keeping customers happy and sticking to the rules?

- Getting results and being true to your own code of ethics?

- Accepting lower standards or doing it yourself?

What would your people highlight as the things you get right?

What would your people highlight as the things you get wrong?

List each member of your staff. On a scale of 1-10 how engaged are they *really* with their jobs. What percentage of their potential are you getting?

What would just a 25% increase mean to them and to you?

What about a 100% increase?

Which of the four mindsets could give you the results you really want? Choose one. Mentally try it on now as you would don a sharper suit. Look at your team through new eyes. With your new map see the new possibilities. You might already be on your way to building that reputation fast, as someone who gets extraordinary results through people.

You've probably guessed that this book operates at Level 4. I hope you chose this one! Its purpose is to install Level 4 beliefs, techniques and behaviours, those that make inspiration a daily habit. Old and inaccurate maps are consigned to the dustbin of history, where they belong. A Level 4 mindset means you'll get the best out of this book and out of each and every one of your staff.

> *"Your greatest decision will be what universe you will live in."*
>
> **Albert Einstein**

Critical Discussion:
What's wrong with Autocratic (Levels 1 & 2) leadership?

Do we really need a science of motivation when we have formal authority? Surely it's simpler and better to just tell 'em? Our people knew what they were signing up for when they joined, so 'do it or else' is not only fair but expected. The rules are there for a reason. So what's the big deal?"

So surely there must be evidence that shows formal authority is best?

Well yes, in some situations:

Classic theory tells us that autocratic leadership gets better results when the situation is either highly favourable or highly unfavourable. Sounds reasonable enough. I wouldn't want to think too hard about how best to service queues of customers eager to pay, whilst only a direct threat would persuade me to jump out of a plane at 15,000 feet. Classic theory also tells us autocratic leadership gives superior results when routine tasks are involved. Again sounds reasonable; if I work on an assembly line I'll be OK with being told exactly what to do and if I'm only thinking of the money, I'll probably prefer clear instructions.

Formal authority isn't bad in itself. Some tasks like dismissals for serious breaches of company policy can only be accomplished this way. Sometimes just getting the job done is an improvement. I would forgive my boss for a curt response to continued errors and missing sections in my reports. I just know they have to be done right.

The problem with formal authority is to rely on it most of the time. Most of us have spare capacity in that our capabilities exceed the demands of the job. Given the chance, most of us would rather do a better job. Detailed instruction removes choice and expression, opportunities for learning and with it the chance of getting satisfaction from the actual doing of the job itself. Such 'intrinsic' motivation is crucial. When jobs are stripped of intrinsic motivation we typically revert to doing the minimum to get by, to get the reward or simply to avoid punishment.

Because professionals typically do much more than is asked of them, most organisations would not function well if people just did the minimum to get by. So detailed instructions, direct orders and threats will hardly create the team of outperformers you long for.

When what we must do exceeds our capabilities the result is anxiety.

When our capabilities exceed what we must do, the result is boredom.

When the two are matched the results can be outstanding.

Matching the two is most easily achieved by giving others discretion over how they do things.   In other words, the opposite to control. Granting autonomy requires trust. Trust is risky but not trusting is far riskier. If you want your people to act with responsibility you first must give it.

But how can control be maintained if someone is not taking charge most of the time? With everyone doing their own thing, surely chaos will reign? For me Covey answers this question best: "The highest form of control is self-control based on moral, not formal authority." So if your organisation works to norms, morals or values that everyone buys into, then workers will operate in harmony with these. Breaking these norms invites self-censorship and censorship from colleagues.

"When mores are sufficient, laws are unnecessary; when mores are insufficient, laws are unenforceable."

Émile Durkheim, sociologist

So why in an age of self-control are we still so reliant on formal authority? Well, we see the world not so much as it is, but as we are. We project our own needs and beliefs on to others. It's those maps again. Formal authority fulfils many of the psychological needs of those who use it. We get feelings of significance and control as our subordinates knuckle down to business. We get feelings of certainty that things will get done to the desired standard. The actual certainty and control might be an illusion but illusions can be addictive.

So what can you do?

Recognise that whilst formal authority has an important place and can get lots of things done, you should really rely on it as little as possible. Think Levels 3 and 4.

Dispense with as many rules and policies as possible. The fear of running into them kills passion.

Encourage the development of powerful group norms or values that favour harmony and high performance in your team – see later. These will minimise the amount of formal authority you will need to exercise.

Chapter 2

Why we leave our jobs

The state of engagement

A recent Gallup survey[2] suggested that only 14% of the Western European workforce were 'highly engaged', meaning they were psychologically committed to their jobs and going the extra mile to make positive contributions. 66% were 'not engaged' meaning they lacked motivation and were unlikely to make such discretionary efforts. The remaining 20% were 'actively disengaged', or in other words, would have been quite happy to work as a saboteur within their own company. Saboteurs leave trails of destruction, often invisible. Turnover, profits, staff retention and morale are the victims. Disengagement costs.

So why do professionals leave their jobs? Often it is for more money but other gripes get higher priorities in exit interview surveys. Here are ten:

1. Relationship with the boss

2. Bored and unchallenged by the work itself

3. Relationship with co-workers

4. Opportunities to use skills and abilities

5. Contribution of my work to the organisation's business goals

6. Autonomy and independence

7. Meaningfulness of the job

8. Organisation's financial stability

9. Corporate culture

10. Managers' recognition of my performance

Source: Susan M. Heathfield,[3] *Human Resources*

Most gripes would appear to be under the control of our immediate supervisor. So the manager is pivotal.

Even when money is cited as the main reason for departure it might just be that disaffected employees are withholding gripes about their boss in order to preserve positive references and because they believe little will change. In turn, managers might be too willing to accept money as an excuse to avoid facing up to the real reasons for the employee's departure. So money could be even less important than we thought.

It's all about the manager

Dissatisfaction with our immediate supervisor features far more strongly at exit interviews than does dissatisfaction with pay and conditions. So what is it that employees like and dislike about their bosses?

According to Investors in People[4] the most admired quality in managers is trusting employees to do the job. Having experience and being approachable also scored highly, as did being well organised. Over half of those who said they work well with their manager are happier at work, while a quarter of them admit to working harder because of this and say they will stay longer in their position.

The most unpopular management trait was failing to reward or recognise employees for good work. Other complaints included being disorganised, failing to motivate employees and a lack of interest in employees' career progression. Three-quarters of workers admitted to gossiping about their bosses' failings behind their backs.

> *"People join companies and leave managers."*
>
> **Eric P. Bloom: President of Manager Mechanics LLC**

From engagement to burnout: When jobs become unfulfilling

Non-fulfilment of important needs despite best effort is believed to lead to classic cases of burnout. Burnout has been described as 'resulting from a prolonged imbalance between *external* effort and *internal* rewards'. In other words, it is the non-achievement of rewards that are important to the individual.

Features of burnout include:

- **Exhaustion** – both mental and physical

- **Cynicism** – demonstrated by lack of trust, blame, criticism, divisiveness, pessimism, negativity, and sarcasm

- **Lack of Professional Efficacy** – doubt in our ability to perform

Job Engagement is seen as the opposite of burnout: an energetic state where we are dedicated to excellent performance and confident of our effectiveness.

Most studies into the causes of burnout have focused on the lack of 'external' rewards like promotion prospects but these rewards mean different things to different people. As we will see, it is the psychological rewards that are truly important and supplying these might be far easier than supplying the promotion.

So what can you do?

The bad news is that most of the time it really is the manager. The good news is that the causes are firmly under your control and if things aren't good there is plenty you can do to change them. If you have already adopted Mindset Level 4 then you are already on your way to making the most of the powerful tools to come. Please read on.

Chapter 3

Money myths

Two great themes have dominated the history of motivation:

1. It's all about the money

2. It's not about the money at all

Both are right but under different conditions. Try paying your people a substandard wage with few prospects of boosting their income. How much positive motivation will you get? Probably none, as their attention shifts to month-to-month survival and to the unfairness of it all. So motivation starts with paying a wage that removes pay as a source of dissatisfaction. People who can't pay the bills will hardly be inspired by the work. Virtually any job that pays enough could lure them away.

The solution is simple: pay your people enough to take money issues off the table. Now they can focus on all the positive stuff. Better still, pay a bit more than your competitors and do it before they catch on.

Thankfully today's professionals can take for granted a wage that takes care of their basic needs and which supports a lifestyle that goes well beyond mere survival. Their workplaces are free from physical pain and danger. They can afford good clothing, shelter and food. Their priorities now concern luxuries their forefathers would have never have even considered. Our theories and practices have moved on accordingly. The M-word still rears its head but now the meaning has changed. Money is a threshold motivator. Once money issues are resolved it quickly loses its power and the positive impact of further pay rises is very short-lived indeed. Deeper motivators like fairness and professional growth start to kick in. Money simply becomes a measure of these.

Richard Laynard in *Happiness lessons from a new society* reports very little relationship between wealth and happiness. Many people in countries in the developing world with low levels of income per capita are just as happy as those in more developed and prosperous nations. Once an income of £15k pa is achieved, further increases don't seem to make people happier.

So throwing money at a problem will not create satisfied workers, but lack of money will create dissatisfied ones.

"Pay explains why people work in the first place but doesn't explain what they will do once they are there."

Christine Doyle, Director of the Professional Doctorate in Occupational Psychology, University of East London[5]

"I pay my people well but more money is still top of their wish list"

Yes that's often true but now you must look beyond what's being said. Relationship gurus tell us that couples rarely fight over the things they say they are fighting about. So it's not really about the trash that hasn't been taken out, but that one party doesn't feel understood and doesn't feel loved.

Likewise when the well paid complain about money it might just be that they feel unappreciated and that their expertise hasn't been recognised.

So what about carrots and sticks?

Yes, they do work sometimes. Frederick W Taylor's (1911) *Principles of Scientific Management*[6] assumed that work was unpleasant and employees would avoid effort if they could. Therefore motivating workers required efficient and simple task definition, and strict supervision with clear and contingent rewards and punishments. Simply put: reward the behaviours you seek and punish those you don't want. We call these *extrinsic* rewards.

In the typical workplace of the early 1900s Taylor probably had a point. He scored some spectacular successes. In one case, redesigning a coal-shovelling task and introducing an incentive scheme increased production more than fourfold. Employers took note; Taylorism caught on and became embedded in the psyche of most corporations. But is it really our nature to be passive and inert, always needing a prod? Or it is more natural for us to be active and engaged? Daniel Pink in *Drive: The Surprising Truth About What Motivates Us*[7] points to the self-directedness of a one-year-old child as evidence of what we are like 'out of the box'. If we are passive and inert then maybe it's the world of work that has made us so.

Today much of Taylor's work reads like classic cases of workplace bullying. It's not surprising that his theories have lost ground to more humanistic ones over the years. The biggest problem for Scientific Management is that it just doesn't seem to work well for the more creative and self-directed tasks that today's professionals do. Indeed, the associated rewards and punishments might even undermine our performance of these tasks – more later.

Taylorism still works when applied to jobs that are well defined, unpleasant and repetitive. So you could use it on the production line where people might hold an instrumental view of work – as merely a tool for earning money. When it comes to numbers of widgets produced, results are more objective and ensuring fairness is much easier. Everyone can be given a more or less equal chance to share in the rewards.

So Taylor's work isn't so much incorrect but partial. It only applies across a narrow range of situations.

So what can you do?

Find better alternatives to carrots and sticks. There are plenty of examples to come.

Chapter 4

Crunchier carrots and sharper sticks: Can they work?

So what happens if we get a bit smarter with the rewards and punishments? Can they be made to work?

The aftermath of Scientific Management is still seen in the corporate search for crunchier carrots and sharper sticks. Witness Performance Related Pay (PRP) schemes. Do they work? Not particularly according to most researchers. Corporate history is littered with failed PRP schemes.

Yes there is some evidence that well-designed schemes can motivate, it's just so difficult to get it right, particularly when applied to the complex, creative and self-directed things that today's professionals do.

So just giving people a chance to 'fill their boots' won't make many happy in the long term. The schemes are difficult to administer fairly and often backfire as employees focus on the unfairness of the scheme. The extra money will come to be expected and then becomes a source of dissatisfaction when it is *not* earned.

Critical Discussion:
What's wrong with Performance Related Pay (PRP) schemes?

PRP seems on the face of it very sensible. To inspire greater productivity and achievement, just pay the most productive people a bonus.

So what could possibly be wrong with these schemes? Alfie Kohn[8], writing in the Harvard Business Review way back in 1993 reviewed the evidence and criticised PRP on several counts:

Reward schemes typically focus on one aspect of performance at the expense of other desirable aspects. In many studies the 'successful' application of extrinsic rewards increased quantity but at the expense of quality. Schemes were difficult to implement fairly so that rewarding one group for high performance impacted negatively on the motivation of other groups. Kohn concluded that extrinsic rewards only achieved temporary compliance, did not motivate, discouraged risk taking and damaged cooperative relationships. He claimed: "Incentives do not create an enduring commitment to any value or action", adding that training and goal-setting programmes had far greater impact on productivity than did pay for performance plans.

Another researcher Steven Kerr[9] described "The folly of rewarding A whilst hoping for B", pointing out that external or 'extrinsic' reward systems tended to focus on outputs that were easy to measure, e.g. quantity of output, whilst less visible and less quantifiable behaviours like creativity and teambuilding were largely ignored to the frustration of those who practised them.

Less considered is the size of the financial rewards on offer compared to the extra effort needed to get them. The increases in pay that accompany outstanding performance can seem negligible and not worth the price to be paid for the unrelenting effort, time away from family and the lack of a personal life. So if the extra rewards can seem so small, then why do people become so uptight about not getting them? Probably because it's more about recognition for a job well done than the extra money.

So what can you do?

The conclusion of both authors was unsurprisingly that most organisations would be better off if they did not relate pay to performance and relied on other means of motivation.

One possibility is that we simply recognise performance at the annual performance appraisal by applying an appropriate grade. Brings us to the next question:

What's wrong with performance appraisals?

The strongest argument for performance appraisals is that we need them to:

1. Reward excellent work – otherwise great employees might become demoralised and leave

2. Flag unsatisfactory performance

Current performance appraisals work best at these extremes. But it's the big grey blob in the middle where the problems occur. Like PRP schemes it's very difficult to conduct these fairly and people who believe they have been treated unfairly might just act out of role or even become saboteurs.

A recent survey by Deloitte[10] showed most organisations did believe appraisals were useful for determining compensation levels and promotion potential. However, only 8% of HR executives felt their existing performance management process drove high levels of business value. 58% believed their process was not an effective use of anyone's time.

Typical gripes for the employee have included:

Unfairness: Most recipients are disappointed with the grade received, citing factors that were beyond their control. The managers are rarely in a position to actually see their employees perform.

Anxiety: Being judged by another. One complained, "I want a manager that helps me improve not one that evaluates me."

Most managers also seem to dislike the exercise, one calling it 'soul crushing'. Other comments have included, "A prescribed appraisal form suggests I'm not smart enough to do the best thing to inspire, coach and develop my people."

So performance appraisals don't seem to be working for most of us.

The system of giving ratings seems based on an old-fashioned view of employment – think Level 1. 'Workers' are ranked on their measured outputs by 'supervisors'. Today's professionals are 'Knowledge Workers' who are difficult to rate objectively. Knowledge Workers become more valuable with time. The greater the mastery and autonomy they attain, the more productive and motivated they become. Expertise and indispensability can bring with it an arrogance that regards judgment by a manager who might not share their professional expertise, ethics and values as an unnecessary affront, an insult even. Managers might then simply pursue a damage limitation exercise whose only positive outcome is the relief that it's all over for another year.

An emphasis on ratings encourages managers to focus on the appraisal not the development. The two don't sit comfortably together. Line managers will find it difficult to simultaneously adopt a facilitative counselling or coaching role to promote development and at the same time a critical assessing stance to arrive at a grade. In turn, those being appraised might not readily accept constructive feedback and development needs if they feel it is going to affect the grade received.

So what can you do?

It is capability development and inspiration that will drive future performance, so why not move the emphasis away from competitive evaluation towards feedback, coaching and development? You would be removing a huge source of perceived unfairness. Perceived unfairness comes from being compared to others who might have enjoyed greater advantages. Perceived unfairness ultimately erodes the perceived link between effort and reward.

If reviews must include ratings as well as development, these really ought to be done at different times and probably by different people.

In today's organisations goals are reset frequently, even weekly. A once yearly or even six monthly review is far too static. Many companies are dispensing with ratings altogether.

Whilst it is probably too early to dispense completely with the appraisal process, it surely must become more developmental, flexible, inspirational and frequent.

Let your people appraise themselves as far as possible. They should know what is expected of them, so hold them accountable for producing the evidence for both results and for high performance behaviours. Tools might include 360-degree feedback and a support network of colleagues that hold them responsible for behaviour change. When trust is high people will be far harder on themselves than you could ever be. The greater their involvement, the more they will accept the process and outcome. The more committed they will be to taking positive action.

Chapter 5

The power of praise: Get it right

So far we have had a 'bloodletting' of the bad stuff that might be weighing your people down. Now is the time to start filling people up with the good stuff. Typically the first 'empty tank' you will find is that of people feeling valued and of playing a useful role in the success of the organisation in which they work. Recall in Chapter 2 the most unpopular management trait was failing to reward or recognise employees for good work.

How much praise should you give?

Back in the 1960s the social psychologist John Gottman[11] conducted a classic piece of research, trying to predict whether a given marriage would end in divorce. His method was to interview couples and simply count the number of positive and negative comments they made to and about each other. Twenty years on, the ratio of positive to negative comments proved remarkably predictive of whether couples would still be together. In fact 94% accuracy was reported. More than five positives to every negative meant couples tended to be still together, but divorce rates increased sharply as the numbers fell below this 'magic' ratio. Appreciation, or feeling valued then is high on most people's wish list in a relationship and it's hard to imagine the employer-employee relationship being any different.

Now consider that a recent Gallup survey in the USA[12] found that fewer than one in three employees had received *any* praise in the previous week and that few managers approach the five to one ratio; how many employees in your company have effectively divorced the organisation, including you? Even worse, are they still 'working' for you?

Most organisations and managers clearly need to circulate more praise, so why don't they? Perhaps they are afraid that more praise in circulation devalues the 'currency', it becomes worthless. Praise takes our focus away from correction and hence control. Surely praise is valued more if it is given sparingly? Or perhaps too many managers just like being seen as 'lean and mean'. We're back to our own insecurities and it's hardly going to inspire our teams.

I've known managers who feared spoiling their people with too much praise and thus blew hot and cold to keep them on their toes. There were weeks when individuals could do no wrong, followed by weeks when they could do no right. Classic animal experiments by the behaviourist B F Skinner and his contemporaries showed that rats given random and unavoidable electric shocks simply find a comfortable corner of the cage and become motionless. Humans effectively do the same thing when praise is rationed and correction inconsistent.

Many of your staff will need regular positive feedback to reassure them they are doing the right things. Fail to supply it and don't be surprised if the good behaviours disappear. *Why am I doing this if no one cares?* In the absence of feedback of any kind, employees might even do counterproductive things just to get some sort of reaction.

The five to one ratio has been shown to apply in a range of situations. Some research suggests that praise effectiveness can fall off sharply when the five to one ratio is exceeded so there might be merit in the argument that too much praise renders it less effective. The reason might be that these higher ratios involve a relaxing of criteria that renders praise less meaningful. People start to doubt the sincerity of it all.

So do you need to get counting so that everyone gets their quota and no more? Well no, the five to one ratio is of course an oversimplification. The quality of feedback also matters and this isn't well researched at all. We are back to our personal experience of what works.

What does quality look like?

Most of us have been on the receiving end of praise that didn't quite hit the spot. I once witnessed a new marketing manager who, eager to extract more effort from the salesforce, tried to harness the power of praise with his audience. His praise amounted to, "You've all done an amazing job with this product so far, but you need to get better."

In a low trust era his words were greeted with more of a grimace than a glow. Attendees gave their verdict in the bar afterwards, "Better than a kick in the teeth but not much better" and "What on earth does he know about what I've done?" and worse still, "The praise was given just to soften us up for a beating." At once I resolved to make my future praising more informed and more specific. Furthermore I would never combine praise with requests for more effort in the same breath.

So giving the praise without the correction could be a good start,

Faye that was brilliant! In fact you are brilliant! Thanks so much!

Well it might beat giving nothing, but such generalised 'fluffy' praise has a habit of becoming less and less effective with use. Faye increasingly doubts its credibility. "Just what is it I'm supposed to be so brilliant at? Does she say that to everyone just to keep us onside?"

Far better to make praise specific, linked to outcomes and hence believable:

Faye I really admired the way you handled that angry customer. When the pressure was on you just kept your cool, asked some great questions and got right to the bottom of what he really needed.

It was so typical of the kind of customer focus you are bringing to the job.

I think we all learned something from watching you and we'll now be growing an account that's vital to our business.

Notice the ingredients:

1.   Exactly what we saw Faye do

2.   The personal qualities that made the difference

3.   The positive consequences for all

It's hard to imagine Faye's morale not getting a boost. Public recognition increases the likelihood that others will follow her example to make the most of their own positive qualities in anticipation that they too will be recognised in this way. Everyone especially Faye now knows just how to get it.

My most inspirational managers always took the trouble to give a proper praising that highlighted my actions, my best qualities and the outcome achieved. Praising and thanks took the form of timely phone calls, voicemails, or verbal recognition at team meetings. My personal favourite was the handwritten card but preference is an individual thing. Why not just ask everyone in your team? Your praise will go much further.

What about the corrective bit?

We might leave correction out of a praising but it's a necessary evil at times. Feedback on how we are doing is so important during the 'goal striving' phase. However, it can have demotivating effects when it tells people they are not achieving their goals. Studies have found unsurprisingly that corrective feedback leads to poorer performance when it reduces self-efficacy or people's belief in their own effectiveness.

So how can you give corrective or negative feedback that maintains or increases self-efficacy and which inspires more productive effort?

Some recent research suggests it's not easy:

Satoris Culbertson, Professor of Management at Kansas State University, (2014)[13] studied the impact of negative feedback by dividing workers into three types:

1. Those motivated by the desire to learn new things

2. Those motivated by proving their worth

3. Those simply trying to avoid failure

All were asked to reflect on negative feedback received at their most recent appraisal. We might have at least expected the first group to respond positively. In fact no one liked negative feedback nor found it an inspiration for learning and growth.

Even if negative feedback demotivates, correction is needed when someone is off track and headed for trouble. I believe that negative feedback or criticism is most useful when there is something to be destroyed, such as a practice that endangers the individual's and company's standing. When there is something to be built, you should encourage not criticise. The problem is that many situations are a mix of the two, time is often tight and a change in behaviour might be urgently needed.

Again, little research has been done on how best to deliver corrective feedback so it's back to the university of experience.

Story time:
The Feedback Sandwich

As a new manager my first training in the art of feedback meant reducing it to a process. You simply found something positive to praise first and which helped the recipient hear all the bad stuff. It could be made to work "even better" when we finished with a positive affirmation about how much we valued the person. What came to be affectionately known as the 'shite sandwich' had arrived.

Most of us persevered with the sandwich but we struggled with it all. It was hard to do it in a non-patronising way. It all too frequently said, "You tried to do something good, but were foiled by your own incompetence, but you're a nice guy and you meant well." Attempts to make the bread tastier by offering encouragement and belief in the other's ability still suffered from the bitter aftertaste of what was in the middle. Often only the bad stuff was remembered. The nice stuff was quickly dismissed, as only there to disguise the real motive of delivering correction. Enthusiastic sandwich users soon found their staff would recoil at the slightest hint of praise, suspecting that correction was about to be given. It all seemed so inauthentic and manipulative. Most of us just went back to following our instincts on building trust and using tact.

Some years later I met a young and very enlightened HR manager who consigned the sandwich to the dustbin of history with the most elegant of statements, "At the end of the day all that really matters is whether you give a shit!" She was right. When coaching my best salespeople I would on occasion see customer calls that weren't up to their usual standard. For those who knew me well it hardly mattered how I gave the feedback. Even a simple "rubbish by your standard" could quickly lead to laughter and new pledges to raise their game. Why? Because they already knew how much I rated them and how important their continued success was to me. I was measured and rewarded according to their success after all.

Giving feedback for your own benefit, to make yourself look good, stands out a mile. If you are seen not to care then no process will help. If you are seen to care then do you really need a process? If you care and your people know it, you get the benefit of the doubt even when clumsy with your correction. Your acts of good faith will have gained you the right to administer it. It's as if all of us have an internal current account. When you give effective praise to your people, when you build trust, when you recognise and fulfil their needs, you build up a positive balance in that person's account. A positive balance allows you to make a withdrawal in the form of special favours or just getting the benefit of the doubt. If you haven't made any deposits into the account and have only made withdrawals, the account has a negative balance and your requests will be met with rejection. Your cheques bounce. Covey calls this the 'emotional bank account'. It's a great metaphor for building trust.

To build up a healthy balance you simply need to know what counts as a deposit in the eyes of the account holder. Simply listening is a good deposit for most, as is delivering on your promises. Uncovering what is really important to the other highlights even better deposits you could make, ones that are highly personal to the account holder. In contrast, most managers I have known have projected their own needs on to their people in order to make effective deposits, giving others what they would have wanted for themselves. I never doubted their good intentions but there are far better deposits that can be made – see later.

So what happens when you simply haven't had the chance to build up a positive balance? Can you still earn the right to give corrective feedback? I recall the first time I worked with a highly accomplished account manager whose day comprised a series of presentations to different customer groups. He assured me that it was fine for me to give him quick-fire corrective feedback on the run between presentations, as there was little time for proper debriefs and coaching. He just wanted me to 'tell it as it is'.

I was wary of giving corrective feedback so directly, largely due to the occasional sulking I'd experienced when obliging others requesting the same. I remembered a technique a trusted training consultant had told me about.

It sounded like:

I really enjoyed that presentation, your product knowledge was excellent. In particular the way you introduced your killer slide really got the audience's attention. Your questions strongly challenged the audience on the wisdom of their current practices and this gained you control of the discussion… and it would have been even better if you had gained agreement from the group as to how they would move things forward now, meaning you get a proper return on your good work.

Notice there were three positives before the negative, which was really expressed as a want; a missing positive that would have really made a difference had it been present. Still a process perhaps but let's be pragmatic, it works well, perhaps because it follows important principles. If you need an acronym to remember it all, let's call it **IPOST**

Imbalanced (not balanced) – Positives outnumbered negatives.

Permission – Was granted upfront. Better still when the recipient requests the skill area that they want feedback on, e.g. questioning skills.

Observed – Seen first-hand and not based on hearsay.

Specific – Focused on behaviour and not a judgment of the person's overall ability or worth. People feel obliged to defend themselves against judgments – unless they're positive of course.

Timely – The permission sought included time, place and content.

Giving feedback a long time after the event tends to invalidate it and it might appear you've been holding a grudge. Time is important when the other is digesting the feedback. Force-feeding feedback and expecting others to process it in *your* timescale does not work. You should also be available to them when they have had time to consider it. Feedback by email is generally a bad idea as it violates most of these principles. Giving tough feedback and walking away looks good in films but it wrecks relationships and renders your feedback null and void.

So principles rule, not processes. Principles start with your intent. Whose good is the feedback for? What behaviour change might be needed? And how will the feedback help? If in doubt write the purpose of the feedback in 30 words or fewer. It will bring great clarity and integrity to the exercise.

Critical Feedback: The 'no go' and 'tread carefully' areas

Have you ever been criticised for something you could not easily change? How did that feel? How useful was it? Such feedback hurts much and changes little: *Your problem is that you have an irritating voice.*

Most of your people's 'weaknesses' are a case in point. Many managers spend too much time 'correcting' their people's weaknesses. If that's ever been done to you, how did it go? Did your boss get a decent return for time spent? In my experience, salespeople who struggled with admin tasks or perhaps strategic thinking never become superstars in these departments when their managers decided to give them a hard time about it. They might have slightly improved in these areas but often at huge cost to their confidence, spirit and the doing of what they were best at: getting out and winning new business.

So would you be better off just working around your people's weaknesses? Probably. You might be able to move them into a more suitable role or even redesign the existing role so that it contains more of the things they excel at. If the role cannot be changed why not get someone else to help with the admin, say, whilst encouraging them to play more to their strengths?

In my past corporate life, bosses who seemed too interested in my weaknesses never gained my trust. Too often looking for that open sore that could be prodded whenever they needed to get control of me. That's how it felt. Far better to ask your people to make more of their strengths. There is simply more mileage in pursuing improvements they will find easy.[14]

Outstanding individuals are rarely well rounded. If they are great at the creative stuff, they will likely detest the routine and procedural stuff. If they have great people skills, then don't expect them to excel behind a desk.

So work around weaknesses where you can, probably by getting someone else to do those jobs. If people simply must improve at some things then you might settle for minimal improvements that raise their performance to levels that don't undermine their strengths. A great salesperson poor at prospecting will need these skills raised to a minimum level unless of course the prospecting can be done by call centre staff.

So what can you do?

Show you care about your people's success. Show appreciation for good qualities, deeds and results.

Ask your people what constitutes helpful feedback and what doesn't.

Ask yourself whose benefit your feedback is for and what changes you are expecting.

Save critical feedback for things that need to be destroyed. Praise when there is something to be built.

Don't invest too much time feeding back on or trying to change your people's 'weaknesses'. Work around them as far as possible by having them spend more time doing what they are best at and by making more of their strengths.

Chapter 6

Intrinsic motivation: Clean energy on tap?

The really positive stuff begins here. In his 2009 book *Drive: The Surprising Truth About What Motivates Us*[7] Daniel Pink highlighted extraordinary examples of workplace motivation that posed very difficult questions for traditional theories of motivation.

Pink presented striking examples of how unpaid volunteers with no one to manage or 'motivate' them can produce superior results to highly paid and resourced employees. Examples included the success of the online encyclopaedia Wikipedia, which triumphed over Microsoft's Encarta, and also the success of the Internet search engine Firefox.

Google and 3M encourage technical staff to spend up to 20% of their time on projects of their own choosing. For both companies, most of their useful ideas originate here.

These findings at first seemed to overturn the laws of 'behavioural physics'. No one stood around figuring out how to motivate these people. No 'rewards' were offered. It just seems that better work was done because the reward was the activity itself. These rewards can be called *intrinsic* as opposed to *extrinsic*. Intrinsic rewards are by their nature more directly related to performance, more under people's control and so more likely to be effective. But just what is it about an activity that gets people excited?

"If you need me to motivate you then I probably don't want to hire you."

Business Leader anon

Intrinsic vs. extrinsic motivation

An important distinction is in order here. There is general agreement in two sources of work motivation: *intrinsic* – originating from within the person or from the task nature, as opposed to *extrinsic* – originating from external rewards and punishments.

Intrinsic motivation happens when you perform an activity for its own sake. It is the doing that is important. The task itself can be a source of stimulation and pleasure as in a hobby. Alternatively the task itself might be tedious but its accomplishment becomes a source of satisfaction. Also you might perform an activity because you believe it is the right thing to do. Examples could be following your own standards of ethics, commitment to goals, group members or to personal values.

Extrinsic motivation happens when an activity is done to attain an outcome that is separable from the activity itself. Like when work is merely a tool for earning money. In recent years the whole idea of extrinsic motivation has been thrown into question when applied to the creative and self-directed tasks performed by today's professionals.

My own research[15] found that when professionals described their own career-related highlights, intrinsic rewards that come from doing the job itself were far more commonly cited as sources of positive feelings than were extrinsic rewards like money and promotion.

The implications are huge. In today's workplace, extrinsic rewards like money, promotion and perks might be unavailable, unsustainable or carry unwanted side effects. Can you just hand out positive feelings instead? Definitely! I will be showing you how.

Can we combine intrinsic and extrinsic motivators?

So we have two types of rewards that we can deploy in the workplace. Surely if we combine these two, an enjoyable task plus a financial incentive, say, we will get an even better result?

Nice idea but it doesn't seem to work.

Critical Discussion:
What's wrong with combining Intrinsic and Extrinsic motivators?

It might seem logical to combine these two kinds of motivator but it seems that intrinsic and extrinsic motivators are not *additive* and might even be *subtractive*.

A number of published studies[16] have shown that intrinsic motivation and the resulting performance were reliably reduced by *adding in* extrinsic rewards like money. This was particularly true for creative tasks. Subjects just seemed to modify their strategy to do just enough to get the reward but no more. Predictably it was creative tasks that suffered most due to this narrowing of focus. Time taken to solve problems like finding new uses for old objects typically *increased*. Whilst the additional rewards usually produced greater effort in the short term there seemed to be a marked loss of motivation and enjoyment in the long term. Those paid to solve problems typically learned less because they chose easier problems.

The authors concluded that the external reward was now perceived as the reason for performing the task so the task itself became less enjoyable. Sounds reasonable. Paying teenagers to tidy their rooms sends a message that the task is unpleasant and ought to be rewarded, probably ensuring they won't do it for free again. Offering our children extrinsic rewards for studying might be catastrophic. Increased pocket money in return for completion of homework will almost always result in more short-term effort but a marked long-term decline in interest. As a healthier alternative we could have them teach us what they have learned. Once learning is inspired by intrinsic rewards, better grades will surely follow.

A number of studies show that paying people to stop smoking, exercise or take medicines produces good results at first, but the healthy behaviour typically diminishes with time and disappears altogether when the incentives are removed.

Even altruistic motives can be pushed aside through financial rewards and punishments. Payments for the donation of blood have reliably *reduced* numbers of volunteers in studies. In trying to ensure punctuality at parent evenings, schools that applied fines to latecomers found that the numbers of late arrivals actually *increased*.[7] In both examples people seemed to believe they were buying the right not to comply, whether it was not donating blood or to be late for an appointment. In the healthcare arena the perverse effect of extrinsic rewards can be tragic. Hospitalised patients have died of thirst as staff pursued performance goals set by their leaders and by governments.

For examples of the folly of rewarding behaviour A whilst hoping for B take professional standards. When extrinsically motivated, many of us will take the quickest route to the desired result even when it means following the 'low' road. If you have worked with sales teams, how often have you seen customer experience sacrificed for short-term results? Experience has shown that setting sales quotas for repair and maintenance staff results almost inevitably in overcharging customers and in unnecessary repairs. Incentives to call on as many customers as possible results inevitably in more calls on poorer prospects that are simply easier to get hold of. High professional standards need intrinsic motivation. By applying extrinsic rewards we endanger these standards.

Where problems have a clear path or procedure to a solution, the destructive effect of extrinsic rewards is not seen. Likewise routine tasks don't seem to suffer either. All easily explained: there is simply little or no intrinsic motivation to be undermined when performing these tasks.

So what can you do?

When tasks require creativity and self-direction, simply look for ways to make the task more enjoyable:

- Give employees choice over what they do and how they do it

- Give a good reason why the task is important

- Recognise the employee's skill, perhaps by having them teach others

- Don't offer any extrinsic rewards like money

But what if the task is tedious, has no intrinsic value and our team of professionals need to 'just do it'?

Mission critical but dull

Here's a dilemma for the inspirational leader. Imagine you have built a highly motivated team, one that runs on intrinsic motivation. Now you have a crisis on your hands requiring extra and unexpected effort from all. The task is pure drudge. Sending out a promotional flyer to all customers perhaps as the usual mailing company could not deliver as per deadline, or maybe an unforeseen stocktake required by auditors.

The dilemma is that you need it done quickly and precisely but it will be heart-sink for the troops. They will have to forgo their evenings and probably their weekend and you don't want to undo all the good work you have done so far.

The work is mind-numbing and hardly likely to inspire anyone.

So what can you do?

You could just tell them, you are the boss after all. Your people would probably comply especially if they thought you might make their life difficult if they didn't. However, their morale and long-term commitment would surely be damaged. At the very least it would be a huge withdrawal from the emotional bank account ensuring that many of your future 'cheques' will bounce. You could ask for volunteers but how many would offer at such short notice?

The best way might be to offer an if-then reward; this could take the form of:

- A special party or event as long as everyone pitches in

- Gift vouchers for whoever participates

- A small payment for every item completed

So carrots in this situation won't hurt and could even help. There is little intrinsic motivation to be undermined.

But what else could we do to help the chances of success in this new age of inspiration?

You could give a rationale why the task is necessary or even mission critical. It might create a sense of meaning where previously there was little.

You could let people complete the task in their own way. State the precise outcome you want by all means. But give freedom over how the task is organised and carried out.

You could emphasise the enjoyable or developmental nature of the task itself. Well no. You must acknowledge the task is particularly boring. This shows empathy and highlights that this is an isolated event and not part of 'the way we do things around here'.

So with a bit of thought, if-then rewards can be introduced to induce special effort when the task is routine and there is no intrinsic motivation to be undermined.

But what if the task were a creative one? Developing a new campaign ad or a promotional event that would really draw the prospects in. One thing *not* to do for creative tasks is to offer an if-then reward. These have been shown clearly to undermine original and artistic thinking, as people just do whatever is needed to win the rewards. So offering a 20% bonus is *not* the way to go. Instead you might give a now-that rather than an if-then reward. In this way the reward is both unexpected and offered only after the successful completion of the task. It could mean a celebration, the throwing of a party. In this way the rewards are less likely to be perceived as the reason for doing the job and hence less damaging to intrinsic motivation.

Some easily applied intrinsic rewards like praise and recognition are less corrosive than cash and trophies. These might take many forms. Drawing attention to your people's positive qualities can be private or public, a phone call, a card, or whatever you think might be most meaningful to that individual or team.

Chapter 7

The rewards your people want most

The more humanistic theories that followed Taylor in the last century like Maslow[17] and Hertzberg[18] have all highlighted the importance of intrinsic motivation or 'higher order needs'. These only became important once certain physical and 'lower order' needs were satisfied. Seems reasonable; none of us would worry too much about our professional growth if we were hungry and the workplace were a death trap. Fortunately, working conditions have improved to the point that intrinsic or 'higher order' needs will predominate most of the time. It is only when our basic needs are threatened by things like contract changes or redundancy that our needs for growth, self-esteem and pride in a job well done might be shelved.

The theories of Maslow and Herzberg remain popular not because of hard evidence but because they are plausible. It does seem that some needs only become important once certain others are met. Equally some things only become noticeable by their absence. A safe working environment is unlikely to inspire us, but just try taking it away! Money as a motivator operates in a similar way.

So if good pay and working conditions don't inspire, what does? What do intrinsic motivators look like? The search for potent intrinsic motivators with mass appeal has occupied researchers for decades. They have emphasised the importance of 'emotive needs' or 'critical states' that individuals will seek out.

Pink[7] argued for the existence for a powerful triad of intrinsic motivators: **Autonomy, Purpose** and **Mastery.**

"Science shows the secret to high performance is our deep seated desire to direct our own lives, to extend and expand our abilities and live a life of purpose."

Daniel Pink, author of Drive

Autonomy is about creating the conditions for your people to do their best work, usually by giving them a long or even a non-existent leash. **Autonomy** means choice and responsibility. Whilst control means mere compliance, **autonomy** means engagement.

"Hire good people then leave them alone."

William McKnight, former 3M CEO

Purpose highlights the difference between a 'mere job' and a 'meaningful cause'. Eradicating a disease or changing the way we shop could be examples. People will often leave lucrative employment for less well-paid positions that offer a more compelling cause.

Mastery is about getting better and better at a job or skill for its own sake.

So could these become universal motivators for the modern professional? They could be ideal for an overhaul of existing rules, roles and maybe a redesign of incentives and recognition schemes.

Schemes to enhance **Autonomy, Purpose** and **Mastery** in the workplace might include:

- Job redesign and enrichment: increasing job importance, complexity and skills needed

- Self-managed teams

- Participation in creating company values, goals and best practices

- Skills training and personal coaching

- Personal budgets for self-development that can be spent on books and training courses

So with a few policy changes you could transform a once depressing workplace. Think back to those people whom you identified in Chapter 1 as being really motivated at work. Chances are they are experiencing most or all of this triad of motivators. Now you can motivate the team through implementing these schemes.

So now there are three powerful intrinsic motivators you can deploy. But why stop at three? More motivators mean more possibilities. What others might we be missing?

My own research project, the Motive Mapping study[15], used in-depth interviews with professionals to uncover 'most motivated experiences'. Participants identified the feelings responsible for their 'career highs'. Seven work-based sources of intrinsic motivation were found. In order of reported frequency these were:

1. Stimulation

2. Purpose

3. Autonomy

4. Contribution

5. Significance

6. Certainty

7. Growth

Stimulation equals interest, novelty, variety, challenge and fun.

Purpose means working towards a worthy goal, creating results that really matter, both to ourselves and others.

Autonomy means having control or considerable discretion over what we do, being given a long leash because we are trusted. It means taking responsibility for a result.

Contribution equals giving support to others which is appreciated and returned. It is about feelings of belonging and connection with like-minded individuals, people who matter to us. Contribution can mean giving something back for the general good. It's often important to those who have already achieved just about everything else and who go on to become philanthropists. Bill Gates is an example.

Significance is about being successful and being recognised by colleagues as such. Recognition matters not just for our results, but for our own unique qualities. We want to know we matter in the eyes of others.

Certainty is about our confidence that we can get a needed result. It means we can predict the outcome of our actions in a risk-laden workplace. Certainty requires trust in our own capabilities and in those we employ. We want to be sure that we can get by, that things work and that we can avoid the bad stuff.

Growth is about becoming masters in our fields, getting better at something worthwhile usually for its own sake. Growth needs to highlight the importance of learning and developing ourselves to become better people.

So we can think of seven key intrinsic motivators rather than just three. More motivators mean more options. More options should mean better results in a wider range of situations.

The Seven Workplace Needs: Key points

1. We might each possess all seven needs but in differing amounts.

2. The importance of motivators or needs like **security** and **certainty** might have been under-represented in the study due to the quest for emotive highs. Both needs would undoubtedly become more important in workplaces where such highs were absent, where there was danger around, when times were uncertain, or when redundancies threatened.

3. Some of the seven needs can be satisfied fully. In particular too much **certainty** bores us, too much **stimulation** overwhelms us. Needs like **growth** and **contribution** in contrast could be pursued continually throughout our lives and might never be fully satisfied.

4. *Unsatisfied* needs are typically the strongest drivers of behaviour. To the inexperienced and ambitious, **significance** in the eyes of one's colleagues might not be fulfilled. **Significance** in this instance could become the most sought-after need. This need might be pursued in healthy ways as in achieving something remarkable or in unhealthy ways by becoming a rebel or workplace bully. **Contribution** needs might be pursued by building healthy alliances that further the organisation's **purpose** or by

forming unhealthy cliques that only serve the interests of the few.

A number of negative workplace behaviours can be difficult to eradicate because they actually meet most or all of the seven needs. Take autocratic leadership – Level 1; the underlying thinking might be:

If I really lay the law down, I know you will do as I say (certainty) which could be just about whatever I choose (autonomy and stimulation). I know what's best for you (purpose). My tough authoritarian stance wins me lots of admirers in this company culture (significance), getting me promotion (growth) and the chance to show other managers the way (contribution and purpose).

Changing this leader's behaviour will be difficult because their style meets all Seven Workplace Needs. Future changes will depend on finding newer and better ways to meet them.

Used together, the Seven Workplace Needs could be used to motivate whole organisations. Such 'universal' motivators are the stuff of inspirational speeches, getting the troops onside, and of powerful company mission statements. Proposals that address all of these needs might be difficult to resist, as there is something in it for everyone. Take a proposal for implementing new technology in the workplace. Using the seven needs you might say:

The beauty of the new system is that you can do your current jobs just as before and in the same way. However, soon you will discover the greater possibilities of the new machines to do it your way, make the job more interesting and ultimately make your life easier. It's a great opportunity for us all to contribute, to work more closely and support each other all the way. It's also an opportunity to grow both your skills and your value to this organisation. We are proud to be chosen as the best unit to pilot this initiative and, as such, we can become an inspiration to other departments.

Probably more inspiring than *We're going to be the guinea pigs for the new machines next week.*

The Seven Workplace Needs explain much and they really exist. It would be hard to apply them to a typical workplace and not get a result. They take us a step closer to motivation mastery.

So what can you do?

Decide which of the seven needs are least catered for in your workplace and whose availability would make the biggest difference.

Design, develop and implement initiatives that give everyone the chance to fulfil these needs. Here's a few:

Stimulation

- Introduce novelty, variety, and new challenges

- Assign a portion of time, say 20%, for people to work on their own projects – as long as the company might benefit

- Match employee roles to their values, interests and abilities

- Encourage employees to develop and redesign their role, increasing the skill level needed

- Introduce job rotation schemes

Purpose

- Increase task significance by showing how the work impacts on the well-being of the organisation, colleagues, customers, and the wider society

- Involve in development of the company and team mission statement

- Assign projects and goals in harmony with employee values

- Involve employees in the 'whats' of goal setting

- Introduce a 'cafeteria' system whereby employees choose the rewards that are most meaningful to them

Autonomy

- Conduct an autonomy audit – do people feel they get the needed control over their jobs to perform them productively?

- Give a long leash – give trust

- Involve everyone in the 'hows' of goal setting

- Remove as many rules, policies and procedures as possible

- Introduce self-managed work teams

- Have employees appraise themselves

- Give accountability for ends rather than means

- Create flexible working arrangements

Contribution

- Introduce employee suggestion schemes; recognise and/or implement the best

- Hold events and exercises aimed at building cohesive teams

- Create buddying and mentoring schemes

- Involve employees in PR initiatives

- Encourage membership of professional bodies to import new ideas

- Introduce and involve everyone in peer recognition and reward schemes

- Give opportunities for individuals to teach their expertise to colleagues

- Give everyone a vote in big decisions

- Hold cross-training initiatives to create awareness and appreciation of colleagues' roles

Significance

- Highlight role models for skills, achievements and company values

- Assign training and mentoring roles to company role models

- Ask for opinions and act on them

- Recognise those that have impacted on company policy, practices and profitability

- Reward skill and achievement with increased autonomy

Certainty

- Develop staff to enhance employability

- Involve staff in the design of procedures

- Give regular updates on how practices are changing, plus previews on what's to come

- Choose 'safe hands' to pilot new technology and methods

Growth

- Assign learning goals to staff with a view to having them teach others

- Give staff responsibility for own role development

- Recognise openness to skill development by giving a budget for training seminars and books

- Set ambitious targets with learning goals

- Introduce job shadowing and mentoring schemes

- Offer career audits and career counselling

- Create well-defined career pathways and hold regular reviews

Critical Discussion:
What's wrong with motivation in the public sector?

To inspire public sector employees do we need to take a different tack? Public workers are often thought of as being lazy and lethargic, having good pay, conditions and job security but still with little motivation to work. One study[19] found that public employees worked fewer hours and showed less commitment to their organisations than their private sector counterparts.

Does this all imply uninteresting jobs, demotivated employees or simply more interest in home life? It does mean that as a manager you have a tougher starting point. To make matters worse, public sector managers frequently claim a lack of means to motivate their employees due to rigid practices that allow little room for manoeuvre. Many of the traditional carrots and sticks are ruled out, ranging from the ability to fire underperforming employees to the offering of substantial bonuses.

It's not just managers that feel the pain. Public sector organisations tend to be more hierarchical in nature so that front-line employees become disconnected from decisions that affect their day-to-day work. In turn this has fostered a management approach that relies more on coercion than on persuasion and involvement. Jobs in the public sector have been said to suffer from too much routine and specificity. Finally, the politicised environment in which public servants work has always been vulnerable to frequent goal changes, impairing perceived abilities to hit targets.

It's not exactly painting a picture of a great place to work, but does it mean that public servants cannot effectively be inspired? It might simply mean that different strategies are needed. It is plausible that public sector employees are motivated by different needs, possibly ones not readily found in the private sector. Traditional thinking favours more intrinsic values: serving others, satisfaction in making a difference, job security, stability and having a supportive working environment have all been reported. The evidence is often contradictory. In the Motive Mapping study[15] few differences were found between public and private sectors in terms of what was desired but public sector values were significantly less fulfilled, particularly for **autonomy**, **recognition**, **contribution** and **certainty**. Some of these shortfalls might reflect a more procedural nature of public sector work and a more hierarchical nature of these organisations.

What we can say is that the need to motivate public servants has never been higher. In today's economic climate they are constantly being called on to achieve more for less. So anything that might lead to increased engagement and lowered strain has to be worth investigating.

So what can you do?

Please read on. Much can be done to deliver what's needed without drastic organisational changes. Most intrinsic rewards can be readily applied regardless of the workplace type. Each chapter to follow will add its own unique value.

"Working hard for something we don't care about is called stress. Working hard for something we love is called passion"

Simon Sinek , Motivational Speaker

Chapter 8

Motive Mapping: Let's get personal

So we now have more than a few intrinsic and fairly universal motivators. Surely if we design a few company initiatives around these, we can get everyone on board? Well not quite… I recall a pharma industry move towards self-managed sales teams back in the 1990s. Think **Autonomy** and **Mastery** in a big way.

Much of the promised 'explosion' of motivation and talent did indeed happen. Some were clearly transformed by their newfound responsibilities and freedoms, driving them to new levels of commitment and growth. Others simply seized the opportunity to pursue their own personal agendas, which at times amounted to very little. More surprisingly, a few individuals with good track records seemed immobilised by their new freedoms. Having little interest in **autonomy** and self-development, they preferred the predictability and security that came from the old ways of working. They simply waited to be told what to do. They waited a long time for the direction they craved and needless to say did not flourish in the new set-up. It all begs the question of how do we inspire these people in a new age of empowerment?

So whilst we can inspire most of the people most of the time, we cannot assume everyone will respond in the same way. To really master motivation it is to individuals that we must turn. Individuals have an irritating habit of wanting things that are absent from our own painstakingly researched motive shortlists.

Sometimes single wants take on a power that goes well beyond what our theories expect. Napoleon is reputed to have said, "I have made a remarkable discovery. Men who will not fight for money will die for pieces of ribbon." The medals he referred to earned wearers the eternal respect of their fellow men. Those for whom respect was everything would risk everything to get it.

Respect is a personal value that hasn't made an appearance so far, but here we have examples of people willing to die for it. So by just relying on our considerable body of research and ignoring individuals we might miss something big. How many more 'must haves' might be out there that have eluded us, effectively under the radar? Your people might already be looking elsewhere for them.

"If a man hasn't found something he will die for then he is not fit to live."

Martin Luther King

Fortunately today's work rarely demands our own sacrifice, nor does being 'motivated' require that work trumps everything else in our lives. It is enough that the job resonates with your people's needs sufficiently to make their time in work both more enjoyable and productive, so that the role becomes a part of who they are rather than a chunk of time they grudgingly trade for money.

Back to incentive schemes; why do so many get it wrong? Simply because every single employee can *choose* whether to put in effort and take action. Motivation is an individual thing and an 'inside job'. Because everyone has different needs, expectations, values, history, attitudes and goals etc., you cannot simply assume what is right for each member of your team. Many managers give their people what they would want for themselves and expect it to ignite their fires. Wishful thinking indeed.

Company policy vs. personal values... and the winner is...

When an organisation's values clash with those of the individuals they employ, the result is stressful and unrewarding for both parties. Most of us corporate veterans have lived through company initiatives that ran counter to the deeply held values of those they employ. I recall an overenthusiastic promotion of a study that compared a company product with its key competitor. A number of the sales staff considered the promotion in breach of their basic principles of ethics and honesty. For these people, inner turmoil resulted which was resolved in various unhealthy ways. Some acquiesced, voicing acceptance at company briefings while giving a different story to customers. Others openly defied the promotional campaign. One or two looked for new jobs. Few made the said product claims with any enthusiasm nor could they be persuaded they were justified. Increased pressure to 'just do it' only increased resistance. The promotion was ultimately withdrawn on realising the harm done to employee loyalty and customer relationships.

So it's not easy to break deeply held values and principles but so easy to break ourselves against them. So why not just harness these for the greater good instead? First we must learn what they are.

Story time:
Meet Frank

Truly great motivators have the personal touch. Corporate folklore recalls legendary individuals in possession of these gifts. Some of us might have been fortunate enough to work for one. Frank was such a leader. He interviewed me back in the 80s for my first 'drug rep' job. Frank's interview technique was simple: find out what really mattered to you and then decide if he could trust you to deliver in the role. His interrogation bordered on the third degree but you didn't leave without getting to the very bottom of what you really, really needed in a job, an honest answer for whether you could have it, and the price you would have to pay to get it.

Frank never forgot what mattered to you. Revered by most, he attracted the loyalty and respect that most leaders crave. A couple of years previously, Frank had quit his job as head of the parent company salesforce to start a new fledgling division. The products were hardly going to set the world alight. His bosses granted him permission to recruit anyone gullible enough to join such a venture. Nearly three-quarters of the existing sales team applied. Frank had the last laugh.

Colleagues joked that most of us would jump off a cliff if Frank required it and assured us it would be OK. In his organisation there was little supervision, few rules, no sales targets, bonus schemes or formal appraisals. Years of service were the biggest factor where promotion was considered and there were plenty of better paid companies out there. The predominant management style was parental – think Level 2. But turnover was less than 5% per annum and sales well above expectations. What was Frank doing that was so right?

I wondered how Frank's career would have panned out in some of the bigger and more 'progressive' companies that have dominated the industry since. He might well have fallen foul of one of the many competency manuals that have come and gone, most of which struggled to capture those elusive qualities that really mattered. It might easily have been a case of 'Does not display leadership potential'.

Three decades later I came across studies suggesting the most potent predictor of someone's job engagement was simply how much they believed senior management actually cared about their personal welfare. It made sense. Even if trust in the immediate supervisor was low, people still felt protected by the system. You show you care when you take an interest in what's important to every one of your people. Your people in turn reciprocate by caring about your goals – simple.

The element of transformational leadership that usually best distinguishes authentic from inauthentic leaders is individualised consideration. The authentic transformational leader is truly concerned with the desires and needs of followers and cares about their individual development. Followers are treated as ends and not just means.

**Bernard M Bass and Ronald E Riggio,
authors of *Transformational Leadership* (2006)**

I was fortunate enough to work for companies that did take employee engagement seriously. An annual or bi-annual survey would highlight those departments that got it right as well as those needing 'special measures'. In retrospect those differences could have easily been predicted by the leaders' attitude to their staff's welfare. The survey question that probably mattered most was consistently absent:

The head of my department cares about me personally

- Please rate agreement

Just one additional question would surely have hastened the departure of one or two department heads I remember only too well. Problem solved.

So our Holy Grail might simply be to find an easy way of uncovering what *really, really* matters to every individual and to find ways of ensuring its provision that will also further the company's goals. Researchers past and present would agree that it's all really a question of the feelings people most want. We can call these feelings 'values'. Values are emotive needs. We are already familiar with these. The triad of **Autonomy, Purpose** and **Mastery** plus the Seven Workplace Needs will all ultimately be *felt* by those in possession. Now we are just concerning ourselves with each and every individual and how they need to feel in order to be happy and productive.

The power of personal values

Personal values are ideal units or building blocks of intrinsic motivation.

Here's why:

All rewards mean different things to different people and will be valued according to the feelings they create. We love people and things for the feelings they give us. Everything an employer provides will eventually be transformed into feelings of some kind for everyone.

It is these feelings that most influence decision making. In management in-basket exercises, participants consistently make decisions in line with their personal values. Career choice is another example. Values will influence which goals are pursued and how strongly.

Motivation theories have increasingly concerned themselves with the question of which feelings or 'critical psychological states' are key to driving work performance. Between them they have cited meaningfulness, responsibility, knowledge of results, achievement, autonomy, purpose, mastery, affiliation, authority, power etc. Researchers rarely agree on which motivators are most important. The importance of each will vary from one individual to the next so why not just ask? We might even discover some new ones.

Sometimes we don't even need to ask. Our people have been feeding us clues about their values ever since we recruited them, maybe even 'shouting' them daily without us hearing. Take their account of the latest holiday, everyone appreciates different things. It might be the wonder of the changing landscape that lures them back year after year, the peace and tranquillity, the cleanliness, the value for money or perhaps the friendships established with locals. Likewise, employees we would rather retain will leave us for different reasons. Had we simply listened we might have been able to fulfil their needs.

*That meant so much to me because it showed you **appreciate** me.*

*When I was overlooked for that project I felt my skills weren't **respected**.*

Some investigative work is usually needed to get to the bottom of just what is really important to everyone. As usual it's better to be curious and proactive rather than wait until your best people tell you at the exit interview.

Critical Discussion:
What's wrong with past research into what drives us?

Most classic research into finding human motivators has been flawed in some way.

Typical shortcomings include:

Thinking bias: Motivation is obviously a feeling, yet instruments to measure it are heavily cognitively biased. They assess thinking rather than feeling. Even when feelings are included in questionnaires the responses may be 'intellectualised' rather than felt, e.g. *I feel fairly satisfied with my job*. As humans we make unconscious decisions with limited rationality so that emotions play the dominant role.

Too general: Many academics believe that classic models of motivation including those of Maslow and Herzberg did not give sufficient attention to individual differences. We can never assume that everyone wants the same things. Wholesale application of these theories in a dysfunctional workplace would still leave many individuals unmoved.

Led by theory: In classic research the researcher defined key human motivators, often based on dubious evidence.

The researcher then looked for proof that those in possession were highly motivated. Individuals typically chose responses from pre-prepared lists. In my experience, this becomes a routine and detached box-ticking exercise where many respond according to how they believe they ought to. Individuals were thus fitted to models rather than models to individuals, resulting in a lack of validity. We simply cannot be sure the motives in question really exist.

Lack of meaningful outcomes: Whilst we know lots about the kind of rewards that lead to job satisfaction, less is known about what leads to more meaningful outcomes like work engagement, productivity and health. It's often unclear whether it's having these rewards that is important or if it's the process of acquiring them that really counts.

So what can you do?

Use the Motive Mapping process. The research[15] addressed all the shortcomings above. It employed highly in-depth interviews with 31 professionals to capture their most motivated experiences. The associated feelings were described in their own words. The feelings or motivators that emerged were therefore validated by the powerful experiences that generated them – an inside out approach. In their own key words participants revealed exactly how they got inspired.

Similar responses like **stimulation** and **excitement, security** and **certainty** were grouped into broader categories to create a shortlist of seven needs that really existed.

The study laid bare what was truly important and debunked the money myth. There was little or no evidence to support

Taylor's theme of the lazy but mercenary worker who must be motivated by financial rewards and punishments. **Stimulation/challenge** was in fact the most sought after of all feelings. Few participants credited their most motivated experiences to extrinsic rewards. Even when promotion and pay increases were mentioned, participants could easily describe internal feelings like **pride** in their skills or **making a difference** to others as being the real source of fulfilment.

Motive Mapping: The steps

First find a quiet retreat for a series of one-to-one meetings with your people.

In low trust environments your people could easily be 'spooked' by a sudden interest in their needs and might just tell you what they think you want to hear. So frame the discussion, gain permission first and give the true reason for your interest. Share your own values and they will reciprocate in kind. It's been said that our deepest desire is simply to be understood, so getting such attention is a reward in itself. Take the time to get this right. When it comes to people, slow is truly fast. It might be the best investment you ever make in that person.

You might say:

As part of my own professional development and to become a better manager, I need to learn more about what makes my people tick, what motivates everyone in effect. Then I can do a better job in making your role more fulfilling for you, giving you more of what you want in a job. This in turn helps me to get the best out of you and ultimately helps me retain your services, which is important to me. I'll need to ask you a few questions about what drives you personally. Is that OK?

The Master Coach:

Great coaches prefer asking questions to giving answers. You will get better results for two reasons:

1. People are more committed to their own solutions. External pressure can be resisted whilst internal pressure by contrast is almost impossible to resist. So asking beats telling.

2. People are not limited by *your* thinking. Their ideas might be better than ours — hard to accept I know, but something we must do in order to become effective coaches. But it is *your* questions that will grow your people's capabilities and attitudes. That's the skill of the coach.

Great coaching questions raise two qualities in your people:

a. Awareness — In this case of those things that could motivate them

b. Responsibility — If it's to be it's up to me

Performance Coach training is beyond the scope of this book but I'll be supplying some useful questions. Until now you might have just preferred to tell people what they ought to want. If that's the case then now is your big chance to change all that. By asking the same questions that master coaches ask, you can get the same results. You have their recipe.

The Master Coach:
Motive Mapping 1:
Find important values

Ask: What would you say is your most motivated experience at work, in your current or maybe a previous role? Perhaps a time when you thought it *doesn't get any better than this...*

It helps to encourage your people to go back into the experience to reconnect with the feelings of that time. So you might add:

Tell me about what was happening from your perspective. What was going on around you?

The better you do this step, the more your people get 'into state', the more authentic are the emotions you capture and the more accurate the information you will have about what gets that person motivated. Now ask:

What made that so motivating for you?

What were you getting feelings of at that time?

And what's so important about getting that feeling?

What does that in turn give you feelings of?

What is important to you about a job? or

What must you have in a job for it to be satisfying for you?

By now you will be building a list of important values. You might still be missing something important so ask:

If you had all of these things that you've just described in your job, and assuming you were sufficiently well paid, what might cause you to leave that job?

The last question might just reveal your employee's most important value. Knowing what would make our people leave tells us how to keep them. Notice how this question takes money out of the picture. We already know that an inability to pay the bills means people will leave regardless of how much they love the job. So a response like *I would leave if the money were insufficient* tells us nothing new.

All rewards are important for the feelings they give us, so when the answers to your questions involve extrinsic rewards like money or promotion, the next question becomes **What feelings does money give you?** That could be **recognition, freedom, security** etc. Such feelings might be far more easily supplied than the money or the promotion. Likewise when employees answer with 'ends values' like **happiness**, **contentment** and **satisfaction**, these tell us little in themselves. Who doesn't want happiness? Continue to ask about the kinds of feelings that create happiness and contentment. **What feelings must you have to feel happy?** You will arrive at a list of 'means values', things that can be worked with.

You will now have a list of values that can be placed in order of priority. Ask your employee to choose their top five in order of importance. If they cannot decide whether one is more important than another then ask:

If you could have only one of these which one would you choose?

For example, let's say you could either have success without recognition or recognition without success. You choose?

> The power of the Motive Mapping method is that it captures the feelings needed by each individual in their purest form. By starting with the 'most motivated experience' we quickly access the most powerful feelings to have. At this point you should see signs of strong emotions: changes in skin tone, posture, their eyes might moisten and they might even lick their lips. Your person has now gone 'into state'. They are now experiencing the original emotions and can give you a detailed and intimate account of what was going on for them. You can be sure these feelings really motivate because they already have done. Once these 'must have' feelings are captured in people's own words, the next step is to turn them into things that can be prioritised, measured and hence managed.

Meet George.

This is how it looks for him:

Values in order of importance:

1. **Integrity**

2. **Success**

3. **Recognition**

4. **Honesty**

5. **Loyalty**

Now you have some insight into what makes George tick.

If George worked for you, here are a few questions you might have and some answers:

Q. How can I make George's job a truly motivational experience and ultimately retain his services?

A. Help him achieve all these things. You must ensure that his job allows him to be **successful** without compromising his **integrity** and **honesty**. Be **loyal** to George and **recognise** his good deeds. These are fantastic deposits for the 'emotional bank account' described earlier.

Q. Could George really have it all?

A. Yes! All five values could pull him in the same direction. But if one value conflicted with the achievement of another there might be problems.

Q. If George wanted to have it all, where might the conflicts lie?

A. Conflict happens when two or more values pull us in opposite directions and with roughly equal force. Difficulties might arise should **integrity** and **success** be put into conflict, as these are strong values, which could be similar in strength. If **success** ever depended on taking actions that ran counter to other values in George's list, like **honesty** and **integrity**, such a difficult choice would cause George bags of stress. He will likely resolve the conflict in favour of his highest value, that is **integrity**, even if it means he cannot be **successful**. So having it all might depend on the organisation's own values and the resulting pressures on George to conform.

Q. How could I get George to leave?

A. Putting his highest values in conflict as in the example above would be a good start. If George cannot realise his highest values like **integrity** and **success**, then he will be on the lookout for a change.

Q. How could I motivate George, say to recruit him to work on a new project?

A. You would need to convince him that this project would help him live his values – **success** and his **integrity** at the very least. Far from being placed in a situation where he might need to compromise these, his **integrity** and **honesty** would in fact be an asset for this job. The high profile of the project will ensure **recognition** for his qualities and good deeds. Incidentally, the colleagues he will be working with are of the most **loyal** and supportive kind.

You will need to use George's own words when motivating him.

Just as a slight misspelling of an email address ensures it will not reach its destination, substituting 'appreciation' for '**recognition**', or 'devotion' for '**loyalty**' means your words might not hit the spot for George and elicit the same feelings. By using George's own words he will always know what you mean even if you don't really know yourself.

The most powerful persuasion comes from the inside. So why not just ask George how working the project will help him achieve what is really important for him? George would surely be unable to resist such an approach. You had better choose that project wisely and present it with no hidden agendas. With values like **integrity** and **honesty**, George will find any manipulation and misrepresentation difficult to forgive.

What does the value look like?

So far so good. But can you assume that when George talks about, say, **recognition**, you know exactly what he is talking about? So if George craves **recognition** for his good deeds, public acclaim at the company conference might be just the thing or might be a huge embarrassment as in *All I really wanted was a call from you to say I did a good job*. You need to understand exactly what ticks that box, what achieving that value looks like for him. **Recognition** might mean a simple thank you for one and promotion for another. Once you know what fulfils the value in question, your employee's criteria in other words, you will know whether it's possible, whether it's desirable and what to do.

So just ask:

How do you know when you have recognition? or **What has to happen for you to feel recognised?** See George's answers below:

Values & Criteria (when I know I have it)

1. **Integrity**: I am trusted by my colleagues

2. **Success**: Others regard me as such

3. **Recognition**: I get promoted

4. **Honesty**: I have nothing to hide

5. **Loyalty**: My actions benefit others

Now George's values can be turned into truly motivational and practical goals because you have much more clarity on what might satisfy him. We also get clearer on the frustrations he might experience.

So when George talks about **loyalty** he means his own. But it's his colleagues' trust that is truly paramount. If George believed he didn't have this he might become very disheartened.

Defining criteria for each value's achievement highlights the frustrations George might experience. George's perceptions of his **integrity, loyalty** and **success** depend largely on the opinions of others. In this respect he is *externally* as opposed to *internally* referenced – their achievement is defined by others. The opinions of others are a bit out of his control, so he cannot really be sure that by doing what's needed he will achieve the required result.

George's measures of **success** are also a bit vague. He probably wouldn't know himself when he had achieved his goal. So for

George there isn't really a defined point where he can pat himself on the back and say *Yep, I'm a success.* You might need to help him define more specific measures of **success** that are under his own control. Successful implementation of all actions in his monthly plan or hitting an achievable sales target might fit the bill.

The *external* criteria for some of George's other values might cause further problems. In a divisive or low trust environment, his pursuit of **integrity** might steer him away from involvement with company initiatives that he truly believed in lest he be perceived as being on the 'dark side' and risking the loss of his colleagues' trust. This might severely limit the choice of projects that you could assign him. One remedy could be to ask George for more *internal* criteria for **integrity** like being true to himself.

Another potential problem for George is that he is probably too specific about what would satisfy his **recognition** needs i.e. promotion.

Highly specific criteria can doom us to a lifetime of frustration. A classic example in life is placing a high value on our own physical attractiveness but one that can only be satisfied by reaching a certain target weight or even having a supermodel body. Such outcomes might be well beyond our reach so the value only becomes something to beat ourselves up with.

So if no promotion is available or if George isn't quite ready yet, then he might just quit in frustration. He could already be looking elsewhere in his quest.

To keep George onside you would need to find other things that can satisfy his **recognition** needs. We might hold him up as a role model, or have him lead a high profile project, but the answer ideally needs to come from him.

The importance of fulfilment

A value's degree of fulfilment is important. Rating fulfilment on each value not only tells us about George's satisfaction levels but what he might still be pursuing. If his appetite for a given value were satisfied then he might seek no more. So let's have him rate his fulfilment of each value between 0 and 10 where 0 = totally absent and 10 = could not reasonably be better. Our clarity takes another leap forward.

Value & Criteria & Satisfaction out of 10

1. **Integrity**: I am trusted by my colleagues (10)

2. **Success**: Others regard me as such (5)

3. **Recognition**: I get promoted (3)

4. **Honesty**: I have nothing to hide (10)

5. **Loyalty**: My actions benefit others (9)

So how satisfied is George overall with his job? **Recognition** and **success** aside, he seems quite happy. Knowing not only what things are important but also their degree of fulfilment opens up the possibility of an ongoing dialogue with George:

- What's most important to you at this time?

- Why have you scored your fulfilment the way you have?

- What would need to happen to significantly improve each score?

- What would make each of them a 10?

Staying in regular touch with your people's feelings is your best way of keeping them.

For those things that are motivating George, our understanding is greatly enhanced. But here the story takes a different twist. Values that are both strong and relatively unfulfilled become key drivers of behaviour. George's need for **integrity** seems fully satisfied on a day-to-day basis so even though it's his number one, it might not inspire him on a daily basis. He might now take his colleagues' trust as a given. Potential troubles lie ahead.

Success and **recognition** could now become the key drivers of George's in-work behaviour. Once his top values are fulfilled, those further down the list start getting his attention. For **integrity** he might now adopt a 'been there done that, what else?' attitude. **Integrity** might only regain its importance once he has lost or compromised it in some way, quite possibly by being overenthusiastic in chasing **success** and **recognition**. This is a real danger for George.

Value conflicts and shifting priorities can be seen in many areas of life. Relationships are an example. Lovers might want the **security** of a stable relationship above everything else but once that is achieved, the need for **adventure** or **variety** becomes a stronger driver. An affair might result which ultimately destroys the relationship and the **security** that was taken for granted. For the errant partner, **security** now reasserts itself as the top priority resulting in a new relationship. The cycle resumes.

To truly serve and retain George you must never let him lose sight of his number one value, his **integrity**. You must help him find ways to achieve unfulfilled values like **success** and **recognition** – ways that enhance rather than compromise his number one. Holding up **integrity** as a team value and recognising George as a role model might be a good start. It might just be the best thing that's ever happened to him at work.

So by asking a few questions you now have a far greater understanding of George. What motivates him, how he is likely to behave, what will get the best out of him and what will make life unbearable for him. We have 'cracked the code' for inspiring George. So instead of simply giving George what you might have wanted for yourself, you now have some powerful options: new buttons to push that you never knew existed half an hour ago. Not bad!

So what can you do?

Don't treat others how you would want to be treated yourself. Instead, do unto others as they would want to be done unto.

Prioritise your people's top five values and determine what their achievement looks like for them.

Help your people realise more of what is important to them.

Ensure that it helps the corporate cause too.

Critical Discussion: What's wrong with fulfilled values?

We can either be in *possession* of the things that motivate us, e.g. money, status, autonomy, or we can be *striving towards* their achievement. Either situation could conceivably inspire us to greater levels of effort and achievement. So is effort inspired most by *possessing* these things or rather is it the process of *acquiring* them that compels us to engage more fully with our duties?

Most researchers have favoured the latter. It is *unfulfilled* values that are seen as truly motivational, provided of course these things are perceived as attainable. So once a value is fulfilled, it might cease to motivate and new and

---

'higher order' needs might be required. The carrot once eaten no longer tempts us.

If motivation were merely a question of having all those things that make us happy then there would be a much stronger link between job satisfaction and productivity. Whilst the two often do go together, the relationship is better explained by high performance causing satisfaction rather than the other way around.

The Motive Mapping study[15] showed that it was *moving towards* important values that were seen as achievable that predicted higher engagement and lower burnout. Fulfilled values might help us retain our people, for better or worse, but it's those rewards that are compelling, attainable but just out of reach that really inspire.

So what can you do?

Score the achievement of your people's highest values out of 10 and determine what getting more looks like to them.

Ensure your people have ample opportunities to earn these extra rewards. They might need coaching to boost confidence in their own ability to get these.

Some personal values might never be fully satisfied: **growth, mastery** and **contribution** could be examples. So these might be instrumental in driving both performance and enjoyment to ever higher levels. When the sky's the limit, there's nothing quite like plugging into a new, fresh and plentiful energy supply.

Chapter 9

Goal setting: Friend or foe?

Goals: Those against

Few New Year's resolutions are ever achieved in spite of the publicly voiced determination to make them happen. One study quotes only 8%.

Goal setting alone clearly does not lead to accomplishment. We wouldn't just set out in our cars with no map, road knowledge or satnav and expect to get quickly to our intended destination. Even with those things in place we might find the destination insufficiently attractive to warrant the hours of driving and the congestion en route.

For most corporate goals, we have destinations, maps, well-worn routes and effectively a satnav. Familiar targets will be assigned, there will be tried and tested procedures for their accomplishment plus information systems that tell us how we are moving towards the goal. Throw in a few incentives, personal accountability and surely achievement is a forgone conclusion?

It rarely seemed to happen that way. In my long experience, no other corporate ritual ever caused more wailing and gnashing of teeth than the annual objective-setting exercise and the sales targets that went with them. The gripes were always the same, *"It's all so unfair." "Beyond my control." "Where did these figures come from anyway?"*

"Why is bigger always better?" "Goals and targets just demoralise us! We all do our best regardless, so why do we need goals at all?" Why indeed?

Six months down the line, interim appraisals came around. Some of those big goals hadn't even been started upon let alone reached. Goals became an unwanted burden, best kept out of sight and out of mind lest they became sticks to beat ourselves with. Goals just set us up for disappointment and so hardly whetted the appetite for further goal setting. Those who did achieve their objectives complained they were only penalised by ever higher targets and expectations. *"So why be a go-getter? Better to keep your head down and have plenty of excuses come appraisal time."* So goals never seemed to inspire the majority.

Goals: Those in favour

All depressing stuff from the detractor camp. Goals are not working. Those in favour argue that significant achievements are invariably preceded by set goals. Examples are easy to find: Sir Edmund Hillary would surely not attribute that first ascent of Everest to 'just walking around'. If we interviewed the CEO of General Motors to ask how they had made it to the top job, we wouldn't expect to hear: *Dunno… I just kept on turning up for work and they kept on promoting me.* We surely don't get those things that we don't focus on unless by accident. On the flip side, those who practise physical and competitive sports tell us that whatever body part we consciously try to avoid damaging will be the one that suffers. As in 'don't think of a purple elephant'. The brain doesn't seem to do negatives. We get what we focus on, for better or worse.

The verdict

Not knowing precisely what you want is *not* OK. Goal setting therefore has potential, but few of us seem to be realising it. Will the latest tools you now have help you realise the benefits?

A time to take stock of what's been covered so far:

- You can find out what's really important to your people

- You know that moving towards these things is more motivational and probably healthier than being mere 'contented cows' in possession of them

- You can determine what activities your people will find meaningful and enjoyable

- You can give your people effective feedback on their success or lack of it

- You can take much of the pain out of goal setting and goal striving, and replace it with positive anticipation

Personal values will be key but let's not forget the company that pays people's wages. You must work with values that are not just personal but 'critical'.

Critical values are those which are both important to individuals and which are associated with high performance. Examples might be **challenge, autonomy, service, trust, mastery**. Critical values are aligned with what Covey[1] calls 'natural laws' that create success and are therefore 'principles'.

Principles operate regardless of whether we use them or not. If they aren't working for you then they are working for your competitors. More enlightened competitors might be using key principles to overhaul you or you might simply be demoralising your own people through ignorance of them. So maybe we just haven't been setting goals properly in the first place. But how best to do it?

Story time:
The Curse of the BHAG

I attended a company-sponsored 'rah rah' seminar back in the early 90s. We were all asked to commit to a **BHAG** – think **B**ig, **H**airy, **A**udacious **G**oal. I went for a Ferrari because it stroked my ego and it seemed like a nice thing to have. I was assured that if I never lost sight of the goal, and kept a picture of my Ferrari on my desk, it would be all mine in record time.

Twenty years on and no Ferrari... I wasn't exactly crushed by my failure, apart from the odd twinge of fear that someone might remember that event and draw attention to my tragic, Ferrari-less existence. But I could just hear it: *Terry, if all that achievement stuff you go on about really works, then where is it? Where is your Ferrari?*

Exposure as a fraud... I got rattled just thinking about it. I badly needed a credible answer and eventually found one: namely that if a goal isn't aligned to one's values then the goal is unlikely to be achieved because there is no real desire behind it. It sounded good, but surely I desired the Ferrari otherwise I wouldn't have chosen it?

The key words are 'real desire'. How much did I *really, really* want that car? Let's check it out versus my strongest life values at the time:

1. Security
2. Wealth
3. Success
4. Family
5. Friendships
6. Health

Taking these in turn:

Would a Ferrari make me feel more **secure**? No way! I would be constantly fretting about where I had left it.

Would a Ferrari increase my **wealth**? Think depreciation of £100s or even £1000s a month!

Would a Ferrari help my **success**? Unlikely – my customers might take offence, questioning my values and my prices.

Would a Ferrari enhance my **friendships**? Hardly – I might be seen as flash and superficial.

Would a Ferrari enhance my **family** life? A two-seater?

Would a Ferrari make me **healthier**? Well I might easily have wrapped it around a tree!

So I had a good excuse for my failure – phew! A Ferrari didn't really tick any of my important boxes. It was just an ego thing. 'Empty goals' are all around us. Those who want promotion might be examples, perhaps seeking a manager role because someone else suggested they should aim for it, or perhaps the kudos appealed. But what if a manager role ticks none of their 'value boxes'? If it does ever happen then the achievement becomes a mirage. The company loses an excellent professional, gains an unhappy manager and maybe an incompetent one at that. Those big hairy audacious goals must be checked out against what's really important.

Sometimes goals pull us in opposite directions. The prospective manager might really get a buzz from leading others but couldn't bear the increased admin involved or the increased corporate pressure to 'toe the line'. Paralysis results. The goal might be pursued in name only with no real commitment shown when the opportunity eventually presents.

Back to my own story, behind the object of my desire lurked fear: fear of the consequences of achieving my goal, fear that I just wasn't up to being the guy that had it all, at least not without the negatives described.

I read some 'evidence' that any goals are better than no goals at all. Extrinsically driven people who set goals around attaining a given level of wealth were more likely to attain that wealth but were still unhappy. Not exactly an endorsement for empty goals then! It only shows the importance of having goals that are aligned to our values.

So what would have been a better goal for me in the story? The perfect solution turned out to be far less glamorous than the Ferrari that was doomed from the outset. Simply moving to a bigger house ticked all my boxes:

Security & Wealth – Definitely, nothing like bricks and mortar

Business success – Having my own office helped

Family & Friends – Extra space equals bigger and better gatherings

Health – My own home gym would encourage me to exercise

No problems achieving that one.

"Success is the progressive realisation of a worthy ideal."

Earl Nightingale

Effective goals: The ingredients

Victor Vroom as early as 1965 set out his now well-established theory on the motivational value of a goal by using the formula **B = V x E** [20]

Where B = Motivational force, V = Valance or desirability of the result E = Expectancy that action will achieve the intended result

So the more aligned a goal to personal values and the greater the belief in its achievability, the more likely an individual is to take positive action to achieve that goal. It makes sense. Individuals who rate their goals as being higher on V and E tend to have greater job engagement and lower burnout.[15] Rather than draining us, pursuing our goals becomes a *source* of energy. Other researchers have showed that clear, challenging, attainable and attractive goals consistently lead to higher effort and performance in a wide range of occupations.

So taking into account the organisation that pays our wages, effective goals seem to meet three criteria:

a. They further company goals: service levels, sales and profits are examples

b. They are credible: people believe they can be achieved with effort

c. They are desirable or meaningful to the employee: they are value based

Most goals assigned by corporations do well at ticking box a), are not so good for b), can be pretty abysmal for c). All a bit unfortunate really because goal effectiveness as a multiple of a), b) and c) is effectively reduced to zero if any of the three components are absent.

Top tips for achievement

Goal clarity counts. The motivating effect of vague and long-term goals is considerably dulled by not knowing whether we are achieving them. A 'big increase' in widget production is far less clear than a '30% increase over last year'.

Think learning goals. Getting an A in Spanish is a performance goal. Holding your own in a Spanish conversation is a learning goal. A learning goal at work might be writing a report or teaching colleagues how to succeed. Researchers have found that those who set learning goals were typically more able to solve unfamiliar problems than those who set only performance goals.

So time spent checking the likely effectiveness of a goal before its assignment is time well spent. As usual it's better to ask questions rather than give answers. Questions change what we focus on and hence how we feel.

Here are a few useful questions that will not only determine but *drive* goal effectiveness:

The Master Coach:
Motive Mapping 2:
Set goals

A few questions you could ask:

- How will achieving this goal benefit you?

- What might happen if you don't achieve this goal?

- What challenges or dilemmas might you face if you did achieve this goal?

Here's another reason why goals might not be pursued with real force, their achievement would present your people with new problems and difficult choices:

- How can you achieve the goal and enjoy the process?

- How can you live your highest values whilst achieving this goal?

- What do you believe you will need to do to achieve the goal?

- What daily standards will you have to live by to bring those goals closer on a daily basis?

- What kind of person will you need to be?

- How confident are you that you can accomplish this?

- Why are you uniquely capable of achieving this goal?

- What skills and capabilities do you have that will help its achievement?

- What extra capabilities or resources might you need to accomplish this goal?

- Where can you get these?

- Who can help you? How will you enlist their support?

- Will achieving this goal be worth the time and effort needed?

- What will tell us we are on track to achieve the goal... or not?

Particularly important are those questions that relate to daily standards and how the process of achievement might be enjoyed and aligned to one's highest values. If daily standards are not maintained and the process is not enjoyed, daily steps to achievement are unlikely to happen. The timer will expire with the goal still a distant dot on the horizon.

Goals for George

Let's revisit George and check what goals might work for him. Imagine there are four projects that you could assign him. How well do they each tick the boxes of George's most important values?

Project 1. A low profile cost-cutting initiative

Value (fulfilment out of 10 in brackets)

1. Integrity (10) ✗

2. Success (5) ✓

3. Recognition (3) ✗

4. Honesty (10) ✗

5. Loyalty (9) ✗

Score = 1/5

This is project heart-sink for George. Whilst he believes he could do it, for him it's simply the wrong thing to do. Even if he could get the right result for all, there would be little recognition to be had. Forget this one.

Project 2. Achieving preferred supplier status for important customer buying groups

Value

1. Integrity (10) ✓

2. Success (5) ?

3. Recognition (3) ✗

4. Honesty (10) ✓

5. Loyalty (9) ✓

Score = 3/5

This one could work. The only downside is that George feels it's not high profile enough. This could be a major drawback for him as his needs for success and recognition are largely unfulfilled. Increasing the visibility of the project could be a real game changer here, making it irresistible for him.

Project 3. Leading on ethical standards or culture change

Value

1. Integrity (10) ✓
2. Success (5) ✗
3. Recognition (3) ✓
4. Honesty (10) ✓
5. Loyalty (9) ✓

Score = 4/5

This one is very likely to work. George thinks it's definitely the right thing to do and just being chosen as the lead person might be recognition enough for him. It might even lead to promotion! He has a few doubts about his ability to succeed here though. With a bit of coaching on George's self-efficacy, this one could be a huge success.

Project 4. Designing a new and fair appraisal system

Value

1. Integrity (10)   ✓
2. Success (5)   ✓
3. Recognition (3) ✓
4. Honesty (10)   ✓
5. Loyalty (9)   ✓

Score = 5/5

This one will most definitely work. It ticks all George's boxes. In particular it is likely to be high profile enough to impact on his less fulfilled values. Very little persuasion will be needed.

So with a little attention to George's strongest values and how each goal might impact on these, most could be made to work. For the first two goals described we might need to bypass George for someone whose values are more aligned. Even for those goals that are definitely aligned for George we might need to help him see just how these connect with what is truly important for him. When that happens he now 'gets it' whereas previously he merely understood what was being asked of him.

"Either you get it or you don't."

Dr Phil McGraw, psychologist and author of *Life Strategies*

There are no grey areas between 'getting it' or not. In my past sales lives, marketers took pride in showing gently rising graphs demonstrating how the amount of product a customer bought increased slowly and steadily with the number of sales calls made. Around five sales calls were needed before mere prospects became good customers. Those that actually did the selling knew this was nonsense. Typically nothing much happened for a few calls, then suddenly business took off sharply. All because the customer had now 'got it' – a flash of insight as to how the purchase positively impacted on something they valued.

Smooth graphs were simply what we got when combining hundreds of individual cases. The customer could easily 'get it' on the first call especially if you discarded the belief that it took five. Likewise you don't need to spend years, months or even weeks building good relationships with your staff. Hit the right spot, set the right goal and they will 'get it' straightaway.

Critical Discussion: How difficult should goals be?

A classic corporate dilemma. Too easy and little effort might be inspired. Too hard and people give up. Disturbingly there is a growing belief that even goals that do improve performance can breed dissatisfaction and demoralisation because we might still not reach the desired standard. Many have even questioned the long-term value of goal setting for this reason.

So our first questions might be: do goals work at all and what effects do they have on those who pursue them?

Two researchers, Locke and Latham, reviewed 35 years of study on the effectiveness of goal setting.[21] They found the following benefits:

1. Goals direct attention and effort towards what is important. When people are given feedback on multiple aspects of their performance, they typically only improve in those areas for which they have goals.

2. Goals energise us. If they are meaningful they inspire greater effort.

3. Goals affect persistence. Goals prolong effort.

4. Goals create efficient use of our resources. We more quickly select the most appropriate knowledge, skills and strategies.

So goal setting can be a worthwhile exercise but the researchers found that it was the *kind* of goal and *how* they were set that really mattered.

So what about difficulty?

1. Specific difficult goals consistently lead to higher performance than 'do your best' goals.

2. More difficult goals tended to inspire higher effort and performance.

   This was only true up to the limits of ability. Above this point increased anxiety or fear of failure typically compromised choice of strategy and the eventual outcome.

The first finding is unsurprising as 'do your best' is vague. There will be a wide range of 'acceptable' performance levels. The second finding appears to conflict with Vroom's expectancy theory: higher difficulty means lower expectation of success, which in turn should mean *less* effort. The contradiction can be explained in the following way:

Higher level and hence more difficult goals are usually more compelling, greater desirability means more effort is inspired. Their achievement therefore delivers superior results. This would account for the association between difficulty and achievement. Just remember it only works if we don't go beyond our people's beliefs about what is possible.

An important finding was that when people set their own goals, those with higher 'self-efficacy' set more difficult goals than expected, were more committed to them and they employed more effective strategies for their achievement. They were also more responsive to negative feedback. Self-efficacy, an idea made popular by Bandura in 1989,[22] is your belief in your own ability to cope. It is the belief you hold about whether or not you can successfully attain a desired level of performance. By building self-efficacy though training and coaching, exposure to positive role models, positive praise and encouragement, you can encourage the setting and achievement of difficult goals. Without self-efficacy, stretching goals and high effort might easily be punished with failure.

So what can you do?

When your people express a desire for extrinsic rewards like money or promotion, determine what they really, really want? Use the Motive Mapping process to check out how the goal aligns to their highest values.

Set goals with a difficulty that is right up to the limits of your people's ability. But only if:

a. The goal is compelling for them
b. They believe the goal can be achieved

Build desirability. Achieve the maximum fit between serving the company purpose impacting on the employee's personal values.

Build self-efficacy in your employees.

Desirability, self-efficacy and the right level of difficulty are best achieved by simply asking your people to set their own goals. Involvement brings commitment. More valued rewards and rewards that are more responsive to effort will be pursued with greater 'intensity' or 'force'. Self-set goals are more meaningful and hence more effective. Unless you sabotage the process by offering extrinsic rewards, self-setting individuals will typically set *more* not *less* difficult goals. Granting **autonomy** makes it happen – it's that long leash again.

Set learning goals for complex tasks. This means people can experience success even when the task goals are not reached. This keeps morale up and the appetite for further goals.

Make manager-set goals effective[21] by providing a rationale for the goal. In particular how its achievement benefits both individual and organisation.

So think **Autonomy**, **Purpose** and **Mastery**.

"Most people fail in life not because they aim too high and miss, but because they aim too low and hit."

Les Brown, motivational speaker

Chapter 10

The 'bad guys': Get the best out of your most difficult people

So far so good. We now have ways and means to inspire most of our people. Motive Mapping works well for those inclined to push ahead with new ideas and initiatives and who need a new focus for their energy. Good for positive people, you might say, but what about the negative guys?

Back in the 1980s my line manager gave me one of his many pearls of wisdom, "Terry, if you become a manager here, the first thing you'll need to know about your team is who you'll need to encourage and who you'll need to kick." The two types of motivated individual he was referring to have since been recognised by popular psychology as needing different tactics, neither involving violence. If you have spent some years in management, you will likely know the trials and traumas of managing the latter kind so it's worth exploring the worldview or 'maps' of these people.

In the last chapter I drew attention to some individuals who were unmoved by corporate efforts to make the workplace a more inspirational place to be. One of these people might be a good place to start. Let's meet Lisa.

The case of Lisa

Lisa had ten years' experience in the sales role and was described by her manager as a past high performer. Her early success was based on hard work, considerable knowledge of her product and disease area, and a knack for building relationships. More recently she had become "a bit of a plodder", having not really embraced the considerable company changes that had landed in recent years. Lisa typically stayed within her comfort zone, sticking to tried and tested ways that had delivered for her in the past and which relied on her great customer relationships. She rarely went the extra mile for better results.

Whilst customers considered her a good ambassador for the company, internally Lisa had become a fierce critic of the latest company efforts to restructure, empower and develop the sales team, saying, "It's still the same job." Her manager confessed, "I'm at my wits end with her. She can always find reasons **not** to do something. She moans about her pay but shuns bonus schemes. The newer and keener members of the team look to her experience and fall readily under her influence, which is worrying."

So what exactly did Lisa value? The Motive Mapping exercise was not an easy one to conduct. Lisa struggled to come up with times when she was positively motivated but found no problem listing things that had *demotivated* her:

- The unfairness of the new incentive scheme

- Youth and ambition were valued more than years of experience

- Company addiction to passing fads, like restructuring and self-managed teams

- The "devastating" uncertainty surrounding recent sales territory changes

"I never knew whether I'd have a job at the end of it"

- No real pay rise for the last three years

- Customers disliked the aggressive style of selling that the company now seemed to advocate – "It's no longer about the patients!"

Thankfully her manager resisted the temptation to 'yes-but' and instead acknowledged and checked her understanding of what Lisa was saying and how she felt. Once she had finished what had been quite a rant, Lisa at least felt heard and was now prepared to listen to what her manager had to say.

Lisa still struggled to find motivational experiences but was now prepared to discuss those 'not so bad' experiences in the job:

- She had had the first of a few good pay rises some eight years ago and the underlying feeling produced was one of **security**

- Her subsequent promotion to Senior Sales Representative showed that **fairness** applied. It would have been an 'outrage' if she hadn't got it

- Good results with one difficult account meant she could defend her way of doing things, the underlying feelings being those of **vindication** – being right – and again **security**

So now what we have from Lisa is a list of pet hates or 'anti-values':

Unfairness	Lack of real pay rises
Not being valued	My abilities are not being used
Fickleness	Company addiction to passing fads
Uncertainty	Not knowing whether I'll have a job
Insecurity	Constant change

Rejection	Customers complain about the current sales campaign

And a smaller and more grudgingly offered list of likes or values;

Fairness	Getting paid according to my ability
Security	I know I can pay the bills
Vindication	When what I do is shown to work

Even Lisa's likes list is a bit defensive. Not much to get excited about in there. Some of us are clearly more motivated by negatives rather than positives. For Lisa it was the negative things that were most potent and by a big margin.

So what was to be done with Lisa? Her manager found her attitude unacceptable and was coming under pressure to 'do something with her'.

Knowing Lisa's pet hates meant the manager now knew where to 'stick the knife' if she had wanted to: if she had devalued much of what Lisa did, treated her unfairly, withdrawn support for pay rises, created constant uncertainty around her role, then Lisa's life would surely have become so intolerable she would have left. But it was hardly the right thing to do and it would have had a negative effect on the rest of the team. Far better to ask how Lisa's true motivation could be unleashed and her considerable talents used.

The importance of motivation direction

To get to the bottom of the last question we need to understand the difference between two different kinds of motivation that might inhabit two different kinds of individuals, recognised by Neuro Linguistic Programming (NLP) and called motivation direction.

If I posed you the question: *Why invest in a pension?*

You might respond in the positive: *I want enough funds to travel the world when I have all that time on my hands.*

Or you might respond in the negative: *I don't want to be poor and have to sell my home.*

One response is about *moving towards* something pleasurable, the other about *moving away* from something painful.

All behaviour can be explained as movement towards pleasure and/or away from pain. Whilst all of us experience both types of motivation, most of us experience one type more strongly than the other. Lisa clearly moved away from things she didn't like, e.g. **insecurity, unfairness** and **rejection**. It is your people's values that most define what is pleasurable or painful for them, which is why these are so important. In Lisa's case it was her negative or move-away values that were strongest.

Move-away people focus on the painful stuff most of the time and so tend to come across as negative and pessimistic.

We do need to take move-away motivation seriously. People will typically move faster and further to avoid pain than they will to gain pleasure. People leave bosses not organisations, so get it wrong and those you'd rather keep might just jump ship before you even realise you've upset them. Consulting with your team and drawing up an effective list of 'things we don't do around here' or ground rules are a high priority for the new manager.

So which motivation type is best, moving towards a place of pleasure or moving away from a place of pain? Well it depends on the job and the situation: Moving away from a place of pain is typically better at kick-starting motivation. Witness Lisa's initial outperformance in the role. At the time, she was a single mum and risked losing her home; she needed to get on her feet fast. She was highly motivated to get out of that painful situation. People will typically do more to avoid loss than they will to gain something of equal value.

So why wasn't Lisa still outperforming? Probably because the pain that once drove her in the first instance i.e. the imminent prospect of losing her home, no longer applied. Yes the workplace was still something of a painful place for her, but it was manageable pain. Her more enlightened manager could now have threatened her position knowing it would motivate her, but Lisa would have probably just raised her performance to a level that just removed the threat, and then have done no more. She would not have been inspired to keep on raising her standard because she had little to move towards.

So those with move-away motivation might simply do the minimum – enough to remove whatever pain is pressing on them at the time. After that there might be no move-towards goals to inspire them to greater heights. 40% of people appear to have a predominantly move-away pattern[23] and a further 20% are equally move-towards and move-away. So we are not just talking about a few odd-ball people here.

How do you motivate move-away people?

Not surprisingly, to motivate those with a move-away pattern your language needs to be somewhat different. Talking of goals to be achieved might sound like a foreign language to them. Instead you might say:

This will help you to avoid…

You'll be able to steer clear of…

We can get rid of…

A change in language will help but success might still be constrained by the nature of the job itself. Sales roles would seem to need a move-towards orientation. Those wanting to top the sales league tables are likely to do better than those who simply fear finishing bottom. There are useful exceptions. Insurance salespeople sell on a message of avoiding the financial pain that unexpected disaster can bring. Some professions are definitely move-away. Medicine seems to favour such a pattern. We want doctors who focus on what's wrong with us, what might go wrong and in getting us out of pain as fast as possible. If you can hardly breathe you wouldn't welcome a discussion with your GP about your health goals. Likewise in the police, preventing crime requires a focus on all the bad things that can happen if certain preventive measures are not taken.

So just as there are move-away people, there are move-away professions.

Should Lisa have been moved into a different role, one that involved troubleshooting perhaps? She might well have done better in such a role but these weren't available. All was not lost for her current role. In a sales environment we might have overlooked the strengths of her motivation direction and so might have been undervaluing her. There is always a role for devil's advocate after all.

But just suppose she really was dragging the team down. Adopting a strategy that threatened Lisa's **security** was unlikely to be the best solution. Even if it inspired more effort, work would have become a most painful and probably unhealthy place for her. If only she could have found some move-towards motivation. Remember all that stuff on **Mastery** and **Purpose**, but how?

Perhaps Lisa's manager could have uncovered sources of move-towards motivation by having Lisa envisage a pain-free existence where insecurity and feeling devalued were banished for good. What would have been the best thing about that for her? What could have brought this about? Embracing change and personal development perhaps. It might just have worked.

What makes people difficult?

Psychologists tell us that difficult behaviours persist for one reason: they are successful for those who practise them. The bully is rewarded by the victim giving in. The perpetual victim gets attached to the sympathy received from others. The non-assertive are rewarded by the reduction in tension that comes with avoiding conflict.

Sometimes managers themselves are instrumental in creating and maintaining difficult behaviour. You create your own experience. I recall individuals who constantly put themselves down, as in "I'm hopeless at this!" Supportive managers usually responded with compliments, confidence building and a slackening of expectations. So these problem people got their reward – at least until their bosses woke up to how their "support" was simply making the problem worse. The self-deprecating behaviour quickly disappeared when the reward was removed.

So when dealing with difficult behaviours just ask yourself what reward your employee is getting from these and what has been your role in creating or maintaining them. Your role is there I assure you. You will now be in a position to change the behaviours by helping your people find productive ways to get the rewards they want or to avoid the things they fear.

So what reward did Lisa get from being negative? She clearly wasn't getting any favours from her manager. She confessed in fact to really enjoying the devil's advocate role, which made her feel **significant**. So there was at least one positive motive. Now if we could just have found more productive ways for Lisa to be **significant** to others we might have been on to something.

The most powerful force for change

People change most when they change their maps. The fastest way to change someone's maps is to change the perception of their roles. Roles are maps in themselves. The wise manager gets the non-cooperative onside by offering a more inspiring view of their role. You might say:

People look up to you as a role model, for leadership on how they ought to behave. You are essential to this team's success. I badly need your support and expertise but I don't seem to be getting it at present.

So could we have highlighted a **significant** role for Lisa that would have made the most of her experience and talents? We might have used her considerable interpersonal skills to help train and support the team in the building of productive business relationships.

By working with roles or 'identities' you can harness yet more powerful forces for change. These are the subject of the next chapter. Could you go even deeper into the psyche of Lisa and George and get really inspirational? Who are they really? What are they really about? And what could they become?

So what can you do?

Find out what your difficult people might be moving away from or avoiding.

Use Motive Mapping to explore their worst case scenarios and the feelings generated.

Show your people healthy and productive ways to avoid the things they fear.

Ask yourself how you and others might be rewarding problem behaviours and change your behaviour accordingly, cutting off the reward if needed.

Help your difficult people find healthy goals that they can move towards.

Chapter 11

Personal identity: Irresistible forces and immovable objects

Story time:
The Scorpion and the Frog

A scorpion asks a frog to carry him over a river. The frog is afraid of being stung during the trip, but the scorpion argues that if he stung the frog, not only would the frog die but he also would drown. The frog therefore agrees and begins carrying the scorpion, but halfway across the river the scorpion does indeed sting the frog, dooming them both. As both are drowning the frog asks, "Why?" The scorpion says, "Because I'm a scorpion and that's what scorpions do... they sting frogs."

Back in the real world most 'identities' appear to involve good intentions even if the outcomes are questionable. Our parents might have defined themselves in terms of the care lavished on us. Such care might have been given regardless of whether the outcome was positive. Perhaps we were prevented from partaking in 'dangerous' activities that would probably have benefited us. Just being caring parents was the goal.

When visiting my native Wales I'm still fortunate enough to experience some really nurturing 'makeshift mums' from my youth, maybe aunties or the parents of school friends, whose role was always to feed me to busting point lest I not grow. I don't exactly need to grow any more, but still, just having eaten is no defence against force-feeding and having my car loaded with extras just in case I get peckish on the two-hour journey home. Good housewives of their era always showed hospitality to guests, usually by putting plenty of food on the table, the more the better. Many still define themselves in this way and to this day.

These stories highlight the power of identity, the kind of person we believe we are and what we perceive our role to be. We feel compelled to act out our identities even when the consequences are questionable: *That's just the way I am.* Examples of harmful identities are plentiful. Defining oneself as a drug addict rather than a healthy and functional individual who once developed a drug habit is a huge obstacle to change.

Throughout life we are regularly transformed by changes in the way we view our identity. When you became a manager, or a parent, responsible for the lives of others, did you not begin to see the world differently? How did your behaviour change? The fastest way to change anyone's behaviour is to simply change the way they perceive their role in the bigger scheme of things. Their identity shifts and so inevitably does their behaviour.

Identity in the workplace

How we perform our jobs is transformed by our identity. If a teacher defines himself by making a difference to his pupils, or a nurse by her devotion to her patients, it will drive their whole behaviour. These identities will likely be expressed regardless of the material rewards (or the lack of them) on offer, probably even under the worst conditions, with little prospect of improvement and with little regard for their own needs.

Sometimes our identities put us at odds with the organisations we serve, as seen in industrial disputes. However, the consequent withdrawal of rewards and threats of punishment by organisations can merely serve to *strengthen* the 'anti-role' behaviour.

Traditional motivation theories struggle to account for these behaviours. We must conclude that motivation is not just goal driven but expressive in nature. Just being ourselves is the goal. We do things because of the kind of person we think we are, or think we ought to be. If work-based identities can entirely negate the effect of employer-introduced incentive schemes, then no wonder so many Performance Related Pay initiatives fail. Professionals will maintain their work identities to the extent that if their purpose became redundant or unachievable most would seek another job.

Identities are forged by our need for consistency: consistency between what we say and what we do, between what we said yesterday and what we say now, what we do here and what we do there. Witness the unflattering words in the English language that describe those who are inconsistent: fickle, shifty, hypocrite, untrustworthy.

Appealing to our sense of consistency gets results. Have you ever made a public commitment about something that you were going to make happen? Chances are you did whatever was necessary lest your inconsistency be exposed for all to see. The wise salesperson asks customers for glowing product testimonials following a successful trial, knowing that afterwards they will feel the need to 'walk the talk' and become prolific users. The public sharing of opinions and intentions massively increases the probability that behaviours will come into line.

The compulsion to act out our identities even when negative can create behaviours that are harmful to both ourselves and others. A victim identity might be reinforced by placing yourself in situations where you can be bullied and let down. Defining yourself as a rebel means you might become rebellious even in the absence of a worthy cause. The rational behaviour of responding to rewards and punishments becomes redundant. Your reward comes from just being you, even if the consequences are dire. Negative identities are thereby self-reinforcing: *I tell it as it is, that's just the way I am and if I get slapped down for that, then so be it.*

So when discovering your people's workplace identities there is always the uncomfortable possibility you might find an agenda that is totally incompatible with that of the organisation. In practice I find this rare but only when you know what lies beneath can you steer that individual towards something more satisfying for both parties. In a few cases it can mean leaving the organisation. If there exists a big misalignment of personal identity and company purpose, as in an anti-capitalist working as a hedge fund manager, then neither individual nor company will be getting much satisfaction from the arrangement.

Non-work identities

Some of your people might have non-work identities in that they do not define themselves by work in any shape or form. Work is simply a means to an end, a means of earning sufficient funds to pursue hobbies perhaps, or support for the real identity of breadwinner. Whilst it is inevitable and clearly healthy that work isn't the be-all and end-all for everyone, a lack of meaning in the workplace doesn't help anything. The job might be unalterably dull, needing enrichment in some way through greater **autonomy,** say, or the job might just be misaligned to your people's values.

The kind of activities pursued outside of work, e.g. competitive sports, charity work, amateur dramatics, might give us clues as to what is missing in their current role. What is the employee getting from that activity that is missing in work? What values aren't being fulfilled? Can the work role be altered so that both the individual and the organisation benefit? After all, clock watching benefits no one.

So how can the power of identities be harnessed for the greater good? As the most potent predictor of what people will do, you must first uncover what your people's identities actually are.

The question that makes the difference

Appealing to people's sense of identity can overcome the strongest resistance. One of my more difficult coaching assignments involved working with the retail accounts team. The customers were buyers for medium-sized chemist chains and it was discounts that clearly ruled. My company majored on service but our prices were 'hopelessly uncompetitive'. One sales call was going nowhere until the salesperson asked a question that changed everything, "How do you want to differentiate yourselves from your competitors in this area?"

The response was a passionate one, "We need to play an integral and valued role in the local healthcare community. For pharmacists to be seen as expert professionals in their own right, not just counters of pills."

Discounts now paled into insignificance next to the professional and patient support our company could provide, support for the identity that meant so much. Getting the business was a formality.

The Master Coach:
Motive Mapping 3: Uncover personal identities

A few questions you could ask:

- What is it you have the strongest conviction about?

- What would you want to be remembered for?

- Who are you? What else are you?

- How do you define yourself?

- What are you about?

- What is the essence of who you are?

- What do you see as your role in the company scheme of things?

Questions to expand identity and explore potential for change:

- What or who is it you would like to be?

- What's your potential role here?

- What could you become given the right inspiration and support?

- What would it feel like to be that person?

- How would becoming that person help you to live your existing values?

- Imagine living all your values at a 10. What would you be doing and who would you be? What would be your role?

- What's preventing you from being that person now?

- So what needs to happen now?

    - What support would you need from whom?

    - How will you enlist that support?

- How will you communicate your new role to others? What will they see?

- What will you need to do on a daily basis to truly become that person?

- How will you be going about your responsibilities?

Sometimes we find positive identities but behaviours that are out of step. Lisa might be an example. Despite her caring nature, her often indiscriminate rejection of company policy meant there were times when she was helping no one: herself, her colleagues and product end users – in this case the patients. Resolving inconsistencies in behaviour requires that we raise awareness of these versus the positive identity. Conflicts will be resolved in favour of the highest power. In other words, our identity.

So if you see anti-role behaviour or personal standards that fall short you might ask:

- How would you be going about things if this were truly who you were?

- How does this kind of behaviour fit with who you believe you are?

So what needs to change?

A happy ending for Lisa

Positive change depends on whether a greater purpose can be found. In our earlier example, what might Lisa's identity be? It turned out she was more 'carer' than 'promoter'. She was truly passionate about the welfare of the end users of her product – patients in this case. She just felt that changes in working practices and overenthusiastic sales techniques meant their welfare was no longer first priority.

Her nurturing outlook extended to the sales team as well, keeping them safe and happy by modelling 'the right way to do things'. It would have been so disappointing if Lisa's passion couldn't have been harnessed productively. In the light of some of the coaching questions above she began to reconsider and change some of the behaviours that weren't furthering her cause. She eventually got an educational role that suited her well. So at last she found something significant to *move towards* and where her qualities were a real asset.

In Lisa's case there was no great misalignment of personal identity and company purpose. After all, what's good for customers is usually good for companies. Mutual understanding of what both parties are about means that synergies can be found where everyone wins.

Sometimes a brand new identity is called for, particularly when 'rogue' or 'anti-role' behaviours are involved – see the story of Sam. These people might need something to *move away* from before they can *move towards* a new role. You might ask: *What will ultimately happen if nothing changes? And how will that affect your cause?*

Positive change isn't always possible. Take someone who gets their thrills from breaking important rules and company norms, effectively saboteurs in their own organisation. Such a great misalignment of values means change is unlikely and the best possible outcome might be that the person departs. Removal of these people will strengthen the culture of the organisation. Company values and those who live by them will be seen to count for something.

Identity change: The story of Sam

Sam was a very capable and experienced salesperson who became a significant problem. His manager told me:

"Sam is potentially my best salesperson but I'm getting less than 50% out of him. He takes pride in letting others know just how little he does. It's damaging to the rest of the team. We've had words but all I seem to have done is drive the behaviour underground."

Sam reluctantly accepted my assignment as his coach. He simply feared worse alternatives like being performance managed. Building trust wasn't easy. Coaching was seen as 'remedial' treatment and I was perceived as being on the 'dark side' – of being part of the management 'plot' to discredit him. When deciding on your trustworthiness, people look first to what they believe is your role and purpose – your identity in other words. For my part it took a lot of honesty, personal disclosure, plus a few deposits into the 'emotional bank account' before *move-towards* values could be uncovered. Here are the findings:

Values, criteria and satisfaction out of 10

1. **Significance:** My opinion counts (6)

2. **Respect:** My assigned work is worthy of my skills and knowledge (2)

3. **Contribution**: When what I bring to the team is valued (4)

4. **Integrity:** My actions are for the general good (5)

5. **Honesty:** I tell it as it is and get the same in return (7)

It's easy to see why Sam so dreaded the threat of performance management. It would have hit him where it hurt most, really 'sticking the knife' into his top three values. Even being singled out for 'remedial' coaching was better. Sam later confessed to being very hurt by not getting the job he really wanted in the recent company reshuffle. He had needed to take a role well beneath his capability. His top three values had taken a big hit and now he looked for ways to re-live them, healthy or otherwise.

Sam's solution was to adopt the role of team cynic, 'helping' the newer and keener members of the team by becoming a model for inactivity. This involved frequent negativity towards company values and demonstrations that team members did not have to swallow the high activity corporate work ethic. What reward was Sam getting from being this way? Possibly by appearing to get by doing so little and by not succumbing to corporate wisdom he would seem smarter than the rest. This would restore some of his self-esteem. Sam actually worked harder than he admitted so there was the clue.

Sam's behaviour might all sound a bit self-indulgent but when work becomes a painful place, people typically look after their own interests and no one else's. Such a dent in Sam's ego meant he would do whatever he could to reverse the damage, even if it meant taking the 'low' road. Was there hope for change?

As for most negative people, the process of change needed to be kick-started by having something to move away from. A few questions around the likely consequences of not changing got Sam's attention. He was clearly uncomfortable not just with the prospect of performance management but also with the self-appointed role of team cynic. He clearly cared about his colleagues, and with nothing to prove personally, really needed to contribute on a bigger scale. Sam's values weren't truly being fulfilled and so he was ripe for a change to a new and more positive identity.

We didn't have to look too far. Sam had often drawn attention to the excessive hours worked by some of the team, sometimes to the point of exhaustion. There was a clear need for a better home/ work balance. Working smarter rather than harder had to be the key. Sam with all his experience and expertise was potentially the perfect champion. Time- and effort-saving practices were second nature to him. Sam could help overhaul the team's working practices so that everyone got more for less – a great working mantra. His manager and I used his own values to sell the idea of how the role could help him achieve what was truly important to him:

"Only you have the expertise to take this role on. You will need to **contribute** everything you know. The **respect** for your experience and capability means your **opinions** really **count** with the team. Your reputation for **honesty** and **integrity** will be a great asset. People will take this project seriously on a national scale. Your **contribution** will go far beyond this team. You would be driving a much needed cause where everyone wins, especially the sales team."

Sam needed little persuasion. As an accomplished salesperson himself, he forgave us for knowing exactly which buttons to push. He even admitted to learning a few new tricks. Two months on Sam was clearly enjoying the new role. The new identity inevitably impacted on his own customer-facing work and sales took an upward swing. Others followed his example.

So what can you do?

Identities come from our values and beliefs about who we are. Provided our values are supportive then new and more powerful identities can be found.

Use the coaching questions supplied to help your people to consider what else they could become and how it might help them realise what's important to them.

If personal values are incompatible with in-role performance then so will be the personal identities. Manage these individuals into suitable roles or out of the organisation.

If a positive identity does not translate into positive behaviour then draw attention to the inconsistency. The errant behaviour will likely be re-evaluated and changed.

Consolidate a new identity by encouraging prompt and consistent action. Identities are forged by consistency so complete the loop ASAP. How will they be acting now? In the absence of new actions nothing will change.

Developing new and powerful workplace identities can be an exciting journey for all. It is these work identities and associated values that can drive performance to new highs regardless of the rewards obtained. It brings us to the ultimate expression of our identities in the next chapter, our personal mission or 'calling' in life.

Chapter 12

Mission critical: The unstoppable power of purpose

Story time:
Your Calling in Life

Back in the early 1980s Steve Jobs ran a fast rising company called Apple. They were highly creative, at the cutting edge of technology but in need of a top manager with an understanding of consumer marketing.

Jobs decided that John Sculley, president and CEO of Pepsi-Cola, was the man for the job. Jobs tried hard to persuade Sculley to join him at Apple. Sculley with all the security, status and financial trappings of his role at Pepsi eventually turned down the offer. But Jobs said something that quickly turned Sculley around. He asked, "Do you want to spend the rest of your life selling sugared water or do you want a chance to change the world?" The rest is history. Sculley realised his life was at a crossroads and discovered his calling in life. Sculley 'got it'.

Our personal mission or 'calling' in life is the ultimate expression of our identities or 'who we are'. It's about our purpose in life or in work. It's about what we want to cause. It is here that identities are turned into a force for good or otherwise. A powerful purpose focuses our entire psychology on creating positive change; these include our identities, values and ultimately behaviours.

In my former 'drug rep' role, the most powerful question I could ever ask an important clinician was: *What impact do you want to have on this condition in your time here?* The deep reflection that often ensued suggested that merely asking the question was a service in itself. When I could show ways of supporting the customer's cause, the relationship was invariably transformed. A partnership was struck, one where both parties gained.

So if only you could find an inspiring purpose for your people and pledge your support, then surely they would be unstoppable…but how? The good news is that they don't all need to change the world to be happy and you can find their purpose simply by looking in the right places.

Help your people find a mission

Uncovering our own mission can be a source of inexhaustible motivation, enjoyment and energy so it's worth investing some more time here. By being aware of your people's identities you are but one small step away.

The Master Coach:
Motive Mapping 4:
Uncover a mission

Some questions you might ask:

For purposes of rapport building it will help to frame the session with a rationale.

You might say:

I want to give you the right kind of support whilst you are in this role so can I ask...

- What are your highest values?

- What mission inspires you?

- What legacy do you want to leave in your current role?

- How do you wish to be remembered?

- What's your vision?

- How will things look when your vision and purpose are achieved?

- What is it you want to cause in this role? And in your career?

- How will achieving your purpose give you what is truly important to you?

- What purpose would help you live all your values at a 10?

Some top tips:

Uncover your own mission before trying this on others.

Use the questions on yourself.

Write the mission statement as though it will never change.

Find a transformative metaphor for the mission. Metaphors transform our beliefs and consequently our actions. They issue constant reminders of what we are about.

> *I'm the lighthouse that illuminates the way in turbulent times*

> *I'm the alarm clock that wakes people up to the opportunities we have to dominate our marketplace*

Ask your people: **How will you make the mission live on a daily basis?**

Maybe a motivational picture or message that sits on their desk, perhaps adopting a mantra or metaphor?

How will you be making important decisions based on your mission?

Outline the dilemmas and important decisions they might have to make in the coming weeks. What does their mission say about how they should resolve them? For example: **As the 'lighthouse that illuminates the way in turbulent times' what role will you be taking in the upcoming company restructure?**

Ask further questions as to how the mission will be lived:

What tasks and activities need to take priority now based on the mission?

How can you accomplish all of these and really enjoy the process?

Which tasks and activities will you need to cut out because they do not relate to the mission?

Mission statements: The benefits

Mission statements focus our energy on what's truly important and so become great time-saving devices; if an activity is not related to the mission then perhaps we shouldn't be doing it. As with identities, rogue or anti-role behaviours can quickly disappear in the context of a powerful mission. The nurse dedicated to the well-being of her patients will quickly reconsider anti-role behaviours that do not further her purpose. She might have a habit of acting independently and neglecting the views of her colleagues. Such mission-behaviour conflicts will be resolved in favour of what is most important, inevitably the mission.

What would be a great mission for George in our earlier example? Maybe to prove that good guys finish first? I'm sure he'd love it but it really needs to come from him. Better work on those coaching questions...

Outperformers: What drives them? Can we create them?

The Holy Grail: Renewable energy

Extrinsic rewards like bonuses, perks and promotion have been described as like using fossil fuels[7]. They might work but they carry with them polluting side effects. One man's gain is another man's sense of unfairness and loss. They become progressively more expensive as the rewards become expected, and their supply more limited. Sustained effort demands frequent top-ups and refuelling.

Intrinsic motivation is like clean power, lacking obvious side effects. Many intrinsic motivators effectively become renewable sources of energy in that they continue to inspire us regardless of their attainment, driving performance onwards and upwards to create ever new highs of performance and motivation. Throw in an inspiring mission and true outperformance becomes possible, inevitable even.

Mastery and **purpose** are effectively renewable sources of motivation.

Mastery means getting better at something for its own sake, approaching perfection in skill but never actually getting there. Total **mastery** lures us simply because it always eludes us. Similarly for **purpose**. If your mission is to make a positive difference to the world at large, to inspire others, at what point do you say enough is enough? Too much **certainty** bores us, too much **stimulation** overwhelms us but when seeking **mastery** and **purpose** you will always crave more. True outperformers run on these. When your employee discovers how growing their own capabilities to pursue company goals furthers their own values and personal mission, you have a new recruit, one that runs on renewables.

A few more questions to create true outperformance:

The Master Coach:
Motive Mapping 5:
Create outperformance

A few questions you might ask:

- How does this task connect with your purpose?

- How can you perform this task in such a way as to be consistent with your highest values?

- How does your level of mastery impact on who you are? And on your purpose?

- What level of mastery are you striving for?

- How will such mastery transform what you do... your mission... your life?

- Should your mission become an unqualified success, what would be the best thing about that?

- What could possibly get in the way of your success?

- How could you ensure that isn't a problem?

One direction: Harness the power of team

"Not finance. Not strategy. Not technology. It is teamwork that remains the ultimate competitive advantage, both because it is so powerful and so rare... A friend of mine... once told me, 'If you could get all the people in an organization rowing in the same direction, you could dominate any industry, in any market, against any competition, at any time.' The fact remains that teams, because they are made up of imperfect human beings, are inherently dysfunctional."

Patrick Lencioni, *The Five Dysfunctions of a Team*

Write a team mission statement

By now you have a good idea of how to elicit personal values and mission statements. Why not do it for your team? It might involve an away day, a day's lost productivity, but it might be the best investment in time you ever make.

There's nothing like a bit of move-away motivation to kick-start a needed initiative. So consider the cost of *not* doing this exercise:

- Lack of awareness of other team members and their motives creates mistrust. Nature abhors a vacuum. We assume the worst about others.

- People feel uncommitted to the values and purpose of the team because they feel their views have not been requested. *Commitment equals involvement.*

- With no clear purpose and values to unite the team, decision making is difficult, confusion sets in around what is the 'right thing' to do. People revert to their own agendas.

- Own agendas typically involve rituals and activities that serve little purpose for the bottom line. Pointless meetings, personal politics, playing safe and appearing to be something rather than doing.

- With no changeless core based on values and principles, people become paralysed by the uncertainty of change.

- Without established norms to keep anti-role behaviour in check, you will need to exercise formal authority more frequently. You will need to apply carrots and sticks to get people focused on the right things.

So compelling are informal group norms and values that they typically exert a more potent and subtle influence over individuals' behaviour than do old-fashioned bureaucratic means of control. Now is your chance to create group norms that favour commitment, enjoyment and high achievement.

The Master Coach: Motive Mapping 6: Create a team mission statement

1. Give the whys for the exercise. You might say: *To create a team that makes success certain, enjoyable, a success to which we all contribute. A team we can all be proud to belong to.*

2. Begin with individuals: What is really important to each team member?

   You might have already done Motive Mapping on a one-to-one and can skip this bit. Otherwise you might brief out the following exercise:

   • Imagine you are at your own retirement dinner

   • You are presented with a very expensive gold watch

   • On the back of the watch are engraved five words that describe what you stood for in your career

   • What five words would you want on the watch?

3. Have the team working in pairs to elicit each other's top five values – see chapter 8.

   Key questions might be:

   • What are they?

   • What does their achievement look like?

   • How much are you actually living these on a scale of 1-10?

4. Each member, including you, shares their own information with the team under the heading: What really motivates me and what I need more of.

   The team agrees how they will support each person to achieve what's really important to them.

5. Look for common values across the team.

   Define **critical values** i.e. those which are both important to individuals and which will also help achieve the team's business goals. Five should be sufficient.

   Examples of **critical values** could be:

   Challenge

   Trust

   Personal growth

   Service

   Support

   Critical values can be called principles. Principles work regardless of whether we adopt them or not. Failing to adopt them means they will work against us, handing our business to more enlightened competitors that do.

   Ask what fully achieving critical values would look like, what non-achievement looks like. What is their fulfilment on a scale of 1-10?

6. The team decides how they will monitor, uphold and recognise these.

7. Now create a team mission statement: Choose and pose some of the questions below and flip-chart the answers.

- How do we want to be remembered?

- How could we help make the world a better place?

- What ultimately do we want to deliver?

- What makes us uniquely capable of achieving our goals?

- How do we want to differentiate ourselves from other teams and organisations?

- What are our dreams about our team?

- What is our burning passion?

- What do we do and for whom do we do it?

- Why do we serve our clients in the way that we do?

- How do we serve our clients in the way that we do?

- Why are we in this industry?

- Why did we start this business?

- What image of our business do we want to convey?

- What could happen in 10 years if we remain totally committed to each other and our goals?

- What do we want to prove?

Now the team is ready to draft a mission statement. Have the team work in subgroups to create suggestions for mission statements that can be rated by the group for their ability to both inspire and deliver the needed results.

Hints

Write a timeless statement – as if it will never need to change.

Keep them short and memorable. One sentence is ideal.

Ensure that the mission statement benefits the team, the customers, and the business. If it only represents one stakeholder group then its inspirational value will be limited.

Check the effectiveness of potential mission statements by asking everyone in your team how they believe it benefits them personally.

Take the time to get this right. The right statement might take weeks to emerge.

A mission statement typically consists of two parts:

1. The 'vision' or 'fruits' of team activity

2. The principles and values that will be lived by and by which the vision will be achieved

We cannot divorce means and ends. The key to one is always the other.

A vision is a compelling image of the destination, so engage as many senses as possible: What will the team see, hear and feel when they get there?

An example mission statement could be: *To create a nurturing environment for the development of leading edge service skills that will delight our customers and keep them coming back for more.*

Some real examples to consider:

Nike: *To bring inspiration and innovation to every athlete in the world.*

Starbucks: *To inspire and nurture the human spirit – one person, one cup and one neighbourhood at a time.*

Chevron: *To be the global energy company most admired for its people, partnership, and performance.*

Amazon: *To be the most customer-centric company in the world, where people can find and discover anything they want to buy online.*

Intel: *Delight our customers, employees and shareholders by relentlessly delivering the platform and technology advancements that become essential to the way we work and live.*

eBay: *Provide a global trading platform where practically anyone can trade practically anything.*

Chapter 13

A great place to work: Create one

Have you ever experienced a great workplace? A workplace that far from draining your energy actually replenishes it? I recall such a time and place, created when two great pharmaceutical companies merged in the late 90s.

Historically the industry had probably operated under the Human Relations mindset – think Level 2. Parental and benevolent are the words that spring to mind. The manager-subordinate relationship had been described as not merely parent-child but parent-spoilt child. We were undoubtedly well paid and well treated, but there were plenty of gripes going around. Throughout the merger process the salesforce had suffered huge uncertainties as old jobs disappeared and new ones were created.

A new and experienced 30-strong sales team was set up in order to breathe new life into a six-year-old anti-epilepsy drug that so far hadn't achieved its potential. The company changes hadn't given me the role I really wanted and so I was steered in the direction of the new set-up. I remember asking myself if it was a dumping ground for people like me, a temporary parking lot for those seeking the exit. Few of us had a clue about epilepsy. Some of us didn't want to be there. We did have an enthusiastic young team of marketers. Just how were they going to inspire us?

Today those fortunate to have played their part speak with great fondness of those times. Almost without exception they are rated as the happiest and possibly most productive time of their careers. A few tears can even be involved. So what turned things around so dramatically?

Well, our leaders quickly held their hands up to their lack of knowledge of the therapy area, inviting contributions and paving the way for a truly open culture. Most specialist knowledge rested with a few members of the sales team. These people were highly prized for their pearls of wisdom. We questioned, listened, and reflected on how our old practices might need to change. Here was a clean slate with no prescribed way of doing things. **Trust** and **autonomy** were inevitable – there was no other way. We just needed to share what was working, and share we did. My voicemail box needed twice-daily emptying from the new nuggets of knowledge, top selling tips and favourable comments from doctors and patients. All contributions were welcome and soon everyone found they had something to bring to the party. What was once daunting ignorance became a steep and exciting learning curve.

We not only drew up a set of patient-centred values but actually upheld them. After all, we had created them. Those who truly lived these values by going the extra mile were nominated by colleagues for special recognition at company meetings. Every day we went about our work driven by the difference we could make to patients and the enthusiastic reception received for our shared learnings and successes. Our enthusiasm quickly rubbed off on customers and sales took a rapid upward swing. The hours were crazy but only because we wanted to put them in.

Why did it all work so well? Well we had **autonomy**, **significance** and feelings of **connection** with like-minded colleagues working on a common cause. Everyone felt they could **contribute** and be **recognised** for that. We had a **purpose** that not only made a difference to ourselves but to our customers and their patients. We were building something truly worthwhile. Epilepsy treatment was both complex and **stimulating.** Our goals were about **learning, growth** and **making a difference** and so were firmly under our control.

Map-wise we reached Level 3 and were knocking on the door of Level 4. Could you do better with your own teams? Yes! Because now we know even better!

How you can create a great workplace

By drawing on the many principles contained in this book you can create a truly great workplace. Here's a summary:

Think value fulfilment rather than carrots and sticks

Material rewards are often unavailable, rarely work for the kinds of tasks professionals do and might even push aside more powerful sources of intrinsic motivation. Instead support your people to achieve important values that are consistent with the organisation's priorities. Motivation by values can almost always be applied, comes without side effects and offers greater potential and possibilities. Hence it is a superior option for motivating key professionals, maximising their health and retaining their services.

Unlike financial incentives whose attainment might reduce the incentive for further effort, value-based rewards effectively become renewable sources of energy as their achievement simply increases the appetite for more – think **growth**, **mastery** and **making a difference**. Standards and performance can thereby be driven up indefinitely with individuals becoming true masters in their fields. Most organisations simply would not function if employees returned minimally acceptable levels of performance simply designed to achieve the rewards on offer.

Find out what individuals value most and what counts as fulfilment

This might need to be built into existing organisational processes like the Personal Development Plan. Motive Mapping looks beneath desired rewards like money and promotion for the positive feelings these provide; these are the things that people really want.

Once the desired feelings are known, there might be multiple ways for providing them. If money is really about feeling **valued**, it might be far easier to show **appreciation** for your employee's qualities than to provide a pay rise that might not be available or appropriate. Dissatisfaction with opportunities for promotion could simply mean a need for **recognition.** Recognising the individual's efforts and abilities could be far easier than providing the promotion and healthier for both parties. Stories of promotions 'gone wrong' are common, when the organisation loses an excellent professional and gains a demoralised and incompetent manager.

So by finding what is really desired we pave the way for creative solutions, increasing both your people's motivation and the likelihood that they will stay. There is always a risk that some individuals' values will be incompatible with in-role performance, in which case these people are probably already unalterably dissatisfied and might be managed into a more suitable role that benefits both them and the organisation.

Some values might be difficult to fulfil. **Security** in times of organisational upheaval might be difficult. Alternatives exist. Personal development that enhances employability and attractiveness to other employers might go some way to addressing **security** needs. In more rigid bureaucratic organisations more **autonomy** might be subject to policy changes at higher levels. Greater **support, perceived purpose** and **recognition** on the other hand are all highly achievable, might cost very little and would go a long way towards motivating staff.

Help your people find a cause

An inspiring work identity and purpose that has significant common ground with company values and mission will create highly committed and contented employees. They don't need to change the world, just achieve something that's worth being remembered for. So create an organisational or team values and mission statement that takes members' values into account. A mission and values statement is a powerful tool to unite and motivate your people by giving a common focus.

Demonstrate how the organisation's values and goals can impact on your employees and vice versa so they see how high performance benefits not just them personally but also the organisation and wider society. **Purpose** is a highly powerful motivator for most professionals. Look for common ground between individuals' values and company goals. If the organisation already has an effective values and mission statement, you will need to make this explicit in order to attract and recruit candidates whose values are aligned with those of the organisation.

Ensure that everyone's values are appropriate for the jobs they do

Move-away and threat-sensitive individuals are unlikely to outperform in entrepreneurial and sales roles but such traits might be a real asset for anyone in a troubleshooting role. Creative individuals with high **autonomy** and **personal growth** needs will have a hard time with procedural roles in hierarchical organisations. Smaller, more nimble and high trust organisations might be far more suitable. Don't make things too hard for yourself by recruiting the wrong people in the first place. Instead ask how candidates' values might sit with the company mission and how new recruits might live their values in your organisation.

Convert critical values into effective goals

Critical values are those which are both important to individuals and which lead to high performance. **Challenge**, **personal growth, autonomy, responsibility** and **trust** are examples. Good management of critical values makes for organisation success. Set value-based goals that inspire and pledge the needed support. Conducting conversations in a facilitative or coaching style with an emphasis on finding employees' own solutions will increase individuals' overall feeling of **autonomy, control, responsibility** and **self-efficacy.**

Let people set their own goals

Commitment to assigned goals is nearly always lower than commitment to self-set goals. Self-set goals are more likely to be aligned to employee values and to be perceived as achievable. If goals are non-negotiable then there is some evidence that assigned goals can be as effective at increasing performance as those that are jointly set as long as sufficient rationale for the goal is provided. The ideal is to have goals that impact maximally on job success, which the individual values and believes are achievable. Greater engagement, enjoyment and lower burnout will result.

Set learning goals

Whenever goals are complex and difficult, learning goals should be set. These are always attainable and are directly responsive to effort. This will work well for employees with high **growth** and **development** needs but especially when the learning goals lead to other valued rewards, e.g. promotion. The setting of learning goals leads to **mastery** which makes the task a reward in itself. Learning goals are much more under individuals' control and will not leave the go-getters empty-handed.

We know goals pursued for intrinsic reasons are more likely to bring happiness than those pursued for extrinsic reasons. Intrinsic goals like **growth**, **mastery** and **making a difference** are also healthier than material rewards. They continue to drive performance to higher and higher levels, long after the latter have ceased to motivate.

Build self-efficacy through praise, coaching and development

Just like learning goals, the building of self-efficacy is crucial to your people's motivation, particularly for difficult, complex and unfamiliar tasks. You will particularly need to maximise people's self-efficacy for self-set goals. Self-efficacy means higher goals and standards will be set and setbacks are more likely to be overcome. The benefits of self-efficacy don't end there. It's been shown that individuals with positive self-evaluations perceive more intrinsic value in their work and these employees will have lower absenteeism and higher performance.

Public servants are often believed to perceive a weaker relationship between rewards and performance. Here it seems even more important that managers set intrinsic goals that are under employees' control. To engage employees in such goals will require managers becoming more expert in persuasion, motivational skills and in coaching to build self-efficacy.

Make fairness an important and explicit value

The importance of fairness cannot be underestimated, as a lack of it will erode the perceived relationship between effort and reward. If effort is seen not to bring rewards but carrying favour with the boss does, then actual behaviours on the job might not be what the organisation was hoping for!

People's appreciation of employer rewards depends on their expectations of what is fair and just. They ask themselves:

Do I have the same opportunity to earn these rewards compared to:

a) my colleagues and b) how easily I earned these in past roles?

Involving your people more in drawing up policies and guidelines around rewards and making them explicit will help ensure justice is seen to be done.

Reinforce organisational values regularly by recognising those who live them

Demonstrate how individuals' values and capabilities are producing better results. Highlighting those that go the extra mile means high performance behaviours can be maintained and modelled for others to follow. Recognition costs nothing, is hugely motivating but underutilised. Time spent identifying staff who go the extra mile is time well spent. Like most value-based rewards, recognition does not need to wait for the annual performance appraisal. You will have much more control of when and how it can be applied and how often. Schemes whereby staff can nominate their colleagues for special recognition serve the joint purposes of recognising outstanding contributions and involving co-workers in team motivation.

Research by Deloitte Consulting[24] suggests that companies with a recognition-rich culture far outperform those that are more punitive or evaluative in nature. When your people feel recognised and valued they will be much more open to feedback and improvement. If all they hear is criticism they will stop listening and look for employment elsewhere.

Survey the fulfilment of critical values periodically to check for shortfalls across the work unit

You can now design and deliver interventions that plug significant gaps. These could involve: job redesign, **recognition** and **participation** schemes, skills training and personal coaching. **Autonomy, challenge, purpose and support** are likely to be critical values so that anything that increases their achievement through effort will further the organisation's goals. Regular updates on their degree of fulfilment will be needed. This could take the form of formal surveys at six monthly or annual intervals supported by more informal questions at your monthly one-to-one meetings.

Move the focus of appraisals towards motivation and development

The whole point of the performance appraisal is to increase performance.

It is capability development and inspiration that will drive future performance. So why not move the emphasis away from competitive evaluation towards feedback, coaching and development? Competitive evaluation leads to perceived unfairness and justifications for not getting the required results. Your people will focus on why the barriers to performance are beyond their control rather than how they might get round them. With a change in content and emphasis your people will focus less on manipulating their grades and more on the opportunities out there for better results. They will increasingly look to you as someone who simply removes the barriers to outperformance: a hallmark of a truly inspirational leader.

Thanks for reading and good luck!

Should you need additional support I can be contacted on:

terry@mindscapeassociates.co.uk

I would love to hear about your success!

Bibliography

1. Covey, Stephen R. (2009) *Principle Centred Leadership*, Simon & Shuster UK Ltd.

2. Crabtree, S., Gallup study:

http://www.gallup.com/poll/165269/worldwide-employees-engaged- work.aspx

3. Heathfield, S. M., 10 reasons why employees quit their job

http://humanresources.about.com/od/resigning-from-your-job/a/top-10-reasons-employees-quit-their-job.htm

4. Investors in People (2013): A modern management crisis? More than one in 10 workers admire nothing about their boss

https://www.investorsinpeople.co.uk/press/modern-management-crisis-more-one-10-workers-admire-nothing-about-their-boss

5. Doyle, C. E. (2004) *Work and Organizational Psychology: An introduction with attitude*, Psychology Press, Taylor & Francis Group.

6. Taylor, F. (1911) *Principles of Scientific Management*, New York: Harper & Brothers.

7. Pink, D. H. (2009) *Drive: The Surprising Truth About What Motivates Us*, CanonGate.

8. Kohn, A. (1996) Why incentive plans cannot work, *Motivation and Leadership at Work*, In Steers, R., Porter, L. & Bigley, G. (Eds.), McGraw Hill International, 512-518.

9. Kerr, S. (1996) On the folly of rewarding A while hoping for B, *Motivation and Leadership at Work*, In Steers, R., Porter, L. & Bigley, G. (Eds). McGraw Hill International, 503-511.

10. Deloitte: Engaging the 21st-century workforce: Performance management is broken. *Global Human Capital Trends 2014*

http://dupress.com/articles/hc-trends-2014-performance-management/

11. Gottman, J. (1995) *Why marriages succeed or fail.* Simon & Schuster.

12. Robison, J., Gallup: In praise of praising your employees

http://www.gallup.com/businessjournal/25369/praise-praising-your-%20employees.aspx

13. Culbertson, C. (2014) Researcher builds a better job performance review, Kansas State University

http://www.k-state.edu/media/newsreleases/feb14/culbertson22414.html

14. Buckingham, M. (2004) *Now discover your strengths,* Simon & Schuster.

15. Hill, D. T. (2012) Job values, engagement and well-being. *Dissertation submitted for MSc. University of Worcester.*

16. Deci, E., Ryan, R. & Koestner, R. (1999). A meta-analytic review of experiments examining the effects of extrinsic rewards on intrinsic motivation. *Psychological Bulletin 125 No. 6,* 659.

17. Maslow, A. H. (1943). A theory of human motivation. *Psychological Review, Vol. 50, No. 4, pp.370-396,* available at:

http://psychclassics.yorku.ca/Maslow/motivation.htm, retrieved 2010–05–25

18. Herzberg, F. (1968). One more time: How do you motivate employees? *Harvard Business Review, January 2003 (reprint), 87-96.*

19. Buelens, M. & Van den Broeck, H. (2007). An analysis of differences in work motivation between public and private sector organisations, *Public Administration Review, Vol. 67, No 1, 65-74.*

20. Vroom, V. (1995) *Work and motivation.* San Francisco, CA: Jossey-Bass.

21. Locke, E. A. & Latham, G. (2002) Building a practically useful theory of goal setting and task motivation: a 35-year odyssey. *American Psychologist, 57, 705-717.*

22. Bandura, A. (1989). Perceived self-efficacy in the exercise of personal agency, *The Psychologist: Bulletin of the British Psychological Society, 10, 411-424.*

23. Shelle Rose Charvet (2010) *Words that change minds: Mastering the Language of Influence,* Kendall/Hunt.

24. http://www.forbes.com/sites/joshbersin/2012/06/13/new-research-unlocks-the-secret-of-employee-recognition/

Appendix

Motive Mapping questions

1. Find important values

What would you say is your most motivated experience at work, in your current or maybe a previous role? Perhaps a time when you thought *it doesn't get any better than this…*

Tell me about what was happening from your perspective. What was going on around you?

What made that so motivating for you?

What were you getting feelings of at that time?

And what's so important about getting that feeling? What does that in turn give you feelings of?

What is important to you about a job? or What must you have in a job for it to be satisfying for you?

If you had all of these things that you've just described in your job, and assuming you were sufficiently well paid, what might cause you to leave that job?

How do you know when you have recognition?

or What has to happen for you to feel recognised?

Questions for ongoing dialogue

What's really important to you?

Why have you scored your fulfilment the way you have?

What would need to happen to significantly improve each score?

What would make each of them a 10?

2. Set goals

How will achieving this goal benefit you?

What might happen if you don't achieve this goal?

What challenges or dilemmas might you face if you did achieve this goal?

How can you achieve the goal and enjoy the process?

How can you live your highest values whilst achieving this goal?

What do you believe you will need to do to achieve the goal?

What daily standards will you have to live by to bring those goals closer on a daily basis?

What kind of person will you need to be?

How confident are you that you can accomplish this?

Why are you uniquely capable of achieving this goal?

What skills and capabilities do you have that will help its achievement?

What extra capabilities or resources might you need to accomplish this goal?

Where can you get these?

Who can help you? How will you enlist their support?

Will achieving this goal be worth the time and effort needed?

What will tell us we are on track to achieve the goal... or not?

3. Uncover personal identity

What is it you have the strongest conviction about?

What would you want to be remembered for?

Who are you? What else are you?

How do you define yourself? What are you about?

What is the essence of who you are?

What do you see as your role in the company scheme of things?

Expand identity and explore potential for change.

What or who is it you would like to be?

What's your potential role here?

What could you become given the right inspiration and support?

What would it feel like to be that person?

How would becoming that person help you to live your existing values?

Imagine living all your values at a 10. What would you be doing and who would you be? What would be your role?

What's preventing you from being that person now?

So what needs to happen now? What support would you need from whom?

How will you enlist that support?

How will you communicate your new role to others? What will they see?

What will you need to do on a daily basis to truly become that person?

How will you be going about your responsibilities?

Change a negative identity

What will ultimately happen if nothing changes?

What would be the worst thing about that for you?

And how will that affect your cause?

4. Uncover a mission

What are your highest values?

What mission inspires you?

What legacy do you want to leave in your current role?

How do you wish to be remembered?

What's your vision? How will things look when your purpose is achieved?

What is it you want to cause in this role? And in your career?

How will achieving your purpose give you what is truly important to you?

What purpose would help you live all your values at a 10?

How will they make the mission live on a daily basis?

How will you be making important decisions based on their mission?

Regarding the dilemmas and important decisions you might have to make in the coming weeks. What does your mission say about how they should resolve them?

As the 'lighthouse that illuminates the way in turbulent times' what role will you be taking in the upcoming company restructure?

What tasks and activities need to take priority now based in the mission?

How can you accomplish all of these and really enjoy the process?

Which tasks and activities will you need to cut out because they do not relate to the mission?

5. Create outperformance

How does this task connect with your purpose?

How can you perform this task in such a way as to be consistent with your highest values?

How does your level of mastery impact on who you are? And on your purpose?

What level of mastery are you striving for?

How will such mastery transform what you do… your mission… your life?

Should your mission become an unqualified success, what would be the best thing about that?

What could possibly get in the way of your success? How could you ensure that isn't a problem?

6. Create a team mission statement

How do we want to be remembered?

How could we help make the world a better place?

What ultimately do we want to deliver?

What makes us uniquely capable of achieving our goals?

How do we want to differentiate ourselves from other teams and organisations?

What are our dreams about our team?

What is our burning passion?

What do we do and for whom do we do it?

Why do we serve our clients in the way that we do?

How do we serve our clients in the way that we do?

Why are we in this industry?

Why did we start this business?

What image of our business do we want to convey?

What could happen in 10 years if we remain totally committed to each other and our goals?

What do we want to prove?

About the Author

Terry Hill is a performance coach and trainer, with over 30 years' experience in the pharmaceutical industry, where he has held a number of sales, management, training and coaching roles in major market leading organisations, winning a number of awards in the process such as Trainer of the Year and Performance Coach of the Year.

A registered Business Psychologist, Terry is currently Lead Consultant at Mindscape Associates. His passion is for motivation and communication skills, which include leadership, coaching, and influencing science.

Terry writes and delivers training programmes for leading organisations across several business sectors. He lives in Kidderminster, Worcestershire.

Terry Hill MSc, DipM, MBPsS

email: terry@mindscapeassociates.co.uk

Lightning Source UK Ltd.
Milton Keynes UK
UKOW06f0520181215

264927UK00011B/175/P